BRISTOL GLASS

BRISTOL GLASS

Cleo Witt

Cyril Weeden

Arlene Palmer Schwind

Published
for

in conjunction with
City of Bristol Museum & Art Gallery

First published in 1984
by Redcliffe Press Ltd.,
Bristol

ISBN 0 905459 56 3

Printed by South Western Printers Ltd, Caerphilly

CONTENTS

FOREWORD

Since A. C. Powell, the last of the Bristol glassmakers, gave his paper to the Bristol and Gloucestershire Archaeological Society in 1924, Bristol's glass has proved an elusive but fascinating subject for both glass enthusiasts and Bristolians. This publication sets out to make available to a wider public the story of an industry which was central to Bristol during perhaps its greatest century, the 18th, and to describe the major contribution which it made to the history of English glassmaking.

We are fortunate in having been able to draw on the expertise of Cyril Weeden, who has long taken an interest in this area and has a formidable background in the glass industry. With the valuable contribution of Arlene Palmer Schwind, the story acquires an important additional perspective, through its location in the wider context of glassmaking in North America. Finally we are particularly pleased to have the opportunity through the generosity of the Bristol and West Building Society, and with the Redcliffe Press, of publishing the City's own collection of Bristol glass, a rare and important group. From this initiative it is hoped that a new momentum will be given to the study of the "very considerable manufactory for many years in Bristol", as Mathews' Directory described the glass trade in 1794.

The publication has been edited and compiled by Cleo Witt, Curator in Applied Art at the City of Bristol Museum and Art Gallery.

Arnold Wilson, Director of the City of Bristol Art Gallery 1984

ACKNOWLEDGEMENTS

We should like to thank the following for their kind co-operation in this enterprise: Mr. Robert Charleston, who gave so generously of his time and knowledge, Mrs. Audrey Godfrey, Mrs. Joanna Lazarus, the two anonymous collectors who have kindly permitted their pieces to be reproduced, the staff of the Central Reference Library, Bristol, and in particular, at the Bristol Record Office, Miss Mary Williams, the City Archivist, and Miss Judith Close; at the City of Bristol Museum and Art Gallery, Paul Elkin, Kate Eustace, David Eveleigh, Francis Greenacre, Helen Jackson, and most especially, Karin Walton; at the Bristol and West Building Society, Sarah Barnes; at the Redcliffe Press, John Sansom; at the Victoria and Albert Museum, Charles Truman; for the photography, Derek Balmer; and for their central contributions and encouragement, Arlene Palmer Schwind and Cyril Weeden.

Note on illustrations

All objects illustrated, unless otherwise stated, are in the collections of the City of Bristol Museum & Art Gallery. Reference numbers refer to the inventories of the Department of Applied Art (prefixed G, N or NX); the Department of Agriculture and Social History (prefixed T or TA) and the Department of Fine Art (prefixed K, M or Mb).

Cover illustration **The 'Oliver Cromwell' Privateer Glass,** probably Bristol, c1757.
Flint glass, diamond and wheel-engraved bowl on a double-series, opaque twist stem: engraved with a privateer ship beneath 'SUCCESS TO THE OLIVER CROMWELL/COMMANDER PAUL FLYN'. N 7834. Ht. 15.8 cm.
Flyn captained the 'Oliver Cromwell' from 11th July, 1757, during the Seven Years War (1756–63). This glass commemorates the commissioning of a private vessel, licensed to trade as a man of war through the issuing of a letter of marque from the government. A group of merchants might thus recoup their losses in wartime by taking prizes of enemy vessels on the high seas.

Plate 1.

Limekiln Lane Glasshouse, by H. O'Neill. c1821.
Watercolour. Unsigned. M3466. From the Braikenridge
Collection.
By this date, the glasshouse was owned by John Nicholas,
an earlier partner of one of the Child family who directed
it in the second half of the 18th century. The 1830s saw

the closure of Limekiln Lane, which had proved successful
until then. A former partner, John Robert Lucas, had by
then founded his own glassworks outside the city at
Nailsea.
See page 53.

INTRODUCTION:

Bristol's Glass Collections, and a New Look at the Non-such Glass Manufactory

Bristol's Glass Collections

THE SURVIVAL of glass is a curious and random business, at its most tantalising in the case of documented pieces. Their scarcity renders it difficult but rewarding to build up a picture of the production in a city such as Bristol. Since its opening in 1905, the Bristol City Art Gallery has attracted gifts of Bristol glass, some of which have stood the test of time and rigorous scrutiny, and has also set out to acquire and borrow Bristol-made pieces. In 1984 its collections consist of two small groups of documented wares from early 19th century glasshouses and a group of unconnected 18th and early 19th century pieces with Bristol associations, presumed to have been made here. They are complemented by a group of the bottles which formed the 'bread and butter' of the industry, which have their counterpart in the Social History collections of the City Museum, and by a few examples of the crown window glass so important a part of production. Finally, the City Museum's Archaeology department holds groups of material excavated as part of the continuing programme of excavation within the City.

Glass-making formed undoubtedly an important ingredient in the highly successful recipe of trade and industry which brought Bristol such prosperity in the 18th century. It both encouraged and benefited from the trade in wine and medicinal water, for instance, as an anonymous note in the catalogue of the Braikenridge Collection of Watercolours nicely expresses it:[1]

> 'It was formerly an observation in Bristol that the City contained as many Glasshouses as Churches & the proportion of business done in this line was very great.'

At its height during the 18th century and early 19th, the industry survived in a modified form until the 20th century. The first half of the 19th century however is most closely documented, furnishing us with the best known Bristol glassmakers, Isaac and Lazarus Jacobs. Their Non-such glasshouse forms the subject of this enquiry, stimulated by some new evidence recently discovered.

A New Look at the Non-such Glass Manufactory

From the mass of documentary evidence which forms the main source of information on Bristol glass, one name stands out, that of Isaac Jacobs.

Most unusually there survive examples of the wares he made, as well as documentation for his business, though the sum total of the evidence is still frustratingly small. A small group of signed pieces distinctively decorated have until now formed the only sure evidence of what Jacobs' glass actually looked like. They are blue, with gilded decoration and signatures, a rare feature of early glass and an indication of the status Jacobs was to claim for his wares. A letter, however, has recently come to light which adds materially to our knowledge of the Jacobs' glass, mentioning new items as well as those already known. Dated 1808, it was written by Isaac's daughter, Harriet, and requests a consignment of glass for her own use from the factory: the list which she includes throws an interesting light on the factory's production.[2]

It is worth summarising briefly the main events in the history of the Jacobs family, from the arrival of Isaac's father, Lazarus, in about 1760 from Frankfurt am Main[3] to Isaac's bankruptcy in 1820. By 1763 Lazarus was commissioning the free-lance painter, Michael Edkins, to paint a sign and to decorate decanters and glasses with gilding for him.[4] By 1771 he was advertising as a 'Glass Cutter', by 1775 also as an engraver, and he also probably acted as a middleman from time to time for other commodities such as cloth.[5] Between 1785 and 1786, Edkins continued to decorate glass for Jacobs,[6] then probably living at 108 Temple Street, as recorded in the 1775 directory, where he took a leading part in the opening of the new Temple Street synagogue in 1786.[7] In 1787 the business was in Avon Street, St. Philip's, and by 1795 he was listed as a 'Glass Merchant'.[8] On Lazarus' death at the age of eighty seven in 1796, the business was taken over by his son Isaac, who appears at Great-Gardens, Avon Street, from 1797, as 'Glass-Manufacturer'.[9]

Under Isaac Jacobs the business prospered, and in 1799 he acquired a house in the fashionable suburb of Kingsdown, at 16 Somerset Square.[10] In about 1804 he took as his apprentice his son Joseph. In 1805 a major expansion took place, described by an imposing advertisement in *Felix Farley's Bristol Journal* for the 'Non-such Flint Glass Manufactory'.[11] A second step in 1806 was to open 'a new set of rooms on purpose for the retail trade', operating at wholesale prices in part.[12] The advertisement of 1806 also mentions 'specimens of the Dessert (set) which I. Jacobs had the honour of sending to her Majesty', perhaps the basis for his claim to be 'GLASS MANUFACTURER to his MAJESTY', incorporated in a contemporary billhead.[13] No evidence unfortunately has yet come to light to substantiate this claim.

Further recognition followed in 1809 with the Freedom of the City, and in 1812 with the grant of a coat of arms.[14] In the same year, after some disagreement, Isaac took his son Joseph into partnership, and he sent Joseph abroad on occasion on the firm's behalf.[15] By 1820, Isaac was in difficulties, partly no doubt due to the economic recession caused by the Napoleonic Wars, intensified for Bristol merchants by the American War of 1812–14. Isaac was in debt, was declared bankrupt, and even for two days jailed for a bad debt of £2,000, for which he had mistakenly stood surety on behalf of a friend who defaulted.[16] The spectacular profits of the early 1810s had vanished, and by 1821 the glassworks had closed.[17]

From this evidence it is possible to form some assessment of the character of the Jacobs' family business, and to suggest an answer to one of the questions raised most often about this enterprise. There has always been a certain ambiguity about the nature of the Jacobs' 'Manufactory'; did they make glass as well as decorate and trade in it? Processing and selling glass on a large scale might well be described as 'manufacturing' at that period: it now seems clear, however, that glass-making did in fact form part of the business.

The beginnings of the Jacobs' glasshouse lay in Lazarus' decision to take his traditionally German skill of cutting glass abroad, and his choice of Bristol as his new home, one of the leading glass centres in England. Early in the 1760s he set up as a decorator in Temple Street, using at least one freelance painter, Michael Edkins, to complement his own skills. By 1771 he described himself as 'Glass Cutter' later adding 'engraver', and by 1793 as a 'Glass Merchant'. When Isaac took over, however, he described himself in the trade directories (1797, for instance) as 'Glass-Manufacturer'. That this was no mere form of words is born out by a pamphlet written in 1821 in connection with Isaac's bankruptcy, published by the Solicitor to the Commission, C. H. Walker.[18] In John Naylor's petition, included in the pamphlet, Isaac is described as 'glass maker, dealer and chapman',[19] while Naylor describes most significantly Joseph's apprenticeship:

> 'the said Isaac Jacobs taught and instructed, or caused to be taught
> and instructed him (Joseph) in the art and mystery of glass-making.'[20]

It is therefore no surprise that Jacobs advertised in 1805 that he 'will continue manufacturing every Article in the Glass Line (even the common articles) of that superior quality, which has hitherto given him the decided preference to any other House in the Kingdom.'[21] It is right therefore to interpret Isaac's billhead also as referring to a working glasshouse, where the note beneath the main design reads 'no discount but for payment in the usual term of credit and no cullet allowed for till received.'[22] Cullet suggests strongly a working glasshouse, since it is the broken waste glass included in the raw flux which forms the basic material heated up in the furnace. Between 1795 and 1797 it seems probable that the character of the business changed, if the description in the trade directories is to be believed.

Our knowledge of the wares which Isaac Jacobs made is slight and understandably dominated by the decorative wares: useful vessels were also produced, as instanced by the 'neatest flint phials' for 'Gentlemen of the Faculty' (that is, for medical use).[23] Lazarus had had decanters and glasses gilded by Edkins, and blue and enamel (coloured) table glass, such as sugar basins, bottles, jars and basins:[24] the latter follow very closely the descriptions of work done for Vigor and Stevens at Redcliff Backs glasshouse by Edkins.[25] We may also assume that the glass cut by Lazarus was table glass, for which cutting became a highly fashionable decoration in the 1780s, heralding the Anglo-Irish period. This tradition was continued by Isaac, who advertised cut and engraved glass 'both useful and ornamental' in 1805, as well as gilded blue glass in the form of dessert sets.

The dessert set was evidently a prestigious product for the Non-such Glasshouse. It was the item chosen for the Queen, according to the advertisement of 1805. Sets or services were certainly the latest fashion, for as Elisa Hald-Steenberg has demonstrated, the first mention of them seems to occur only two years earlier.[26] In the *Englische Miscellen* of 1803 appears this description:

> 'A service of cut glass, which has now become the fashion on the dessert-tables of the great in England, surpasses any gold or silver both in appearance and in price.'

The last phrase picks up neatly Jacobs' phrase in his advertisement, pricing dessert sets from fifteen guineas per set 'to any amount'.

As profitable as the fashionable dessert sets were probably the personally decorated armorial services bearing 'Coats of Arms, Crests and Cyphers . . . in the greatest style, by some of the First Artists in the Kingdom', advertised in 1805. They were a feature also of the ceramic trade of the period, and Bristol dealers commissioned creamware with armorials in quantity from Josiah Wedgwood, for instance.[27] A fine example from the Non-such Glasshouse survives in the decanter stand or dish in the City of Bristol Museum and Art Gallery as N 2031 (see plate

22). From the same date probably come the other signed and similarly decorated pieces of this type: decanters, fingerbowls and wine-glass coolers (see plates 21, 23 and 24).

We must now return to the letter sent by Harriet Keyser, née Jacobs, and look at her list of requests in the light of the products of the Non-such glasshouse, as it can now legitimately be called.

Mr. David Samuel   (post mark: JU/10/C/808, i.e. June 10th 1808)
Mrs. Jacobs
Glass Manufactory
Bristol

My Dear Punch,
I dare say you have spoild th( ) Beautiful dear little face of yours about a Dozen times since I have been gone because I did not Write to you, I hope you have had little Eyes lately then I am sure you are good temper'd, you were kind enough to promise me faithfully (& I know I can depend on you) to send me some Glass which we are very much in want of – Please God the 24th June we are going to have a large party to Dinner if you do not sent it before then you never shall have a kiss of me any more your own Darling – D(--- --ar), & I am sure you would break your heart the 24th you must have little Eyes as it was that day twelvemonth I was married even my Dear Granny must get Tipsy God Bless her give my Love & Duty to her tell her I long to have a kiss of her my love to (?) Jac my Dear Keyser desires his Compliments to you Papa is Thank God very well God Bless you and keep with you and your Dripping Pan my Dear Davy. I

remain your sincere Friend

H Keyser

1 Stand for Jelly or any other Glasses in the middle of the Table

2 Doz Good cut Bonnet Rummers

2 Do Cut Lemonades

2 Do Do Jelly Glasses

½ Do Blue & Gilt Edge Wine Coolers

½ Do Do finger Cups

1 Pr Quart Decanters to match the last sent

2 Pr Pint Do

1 Do Champagne Glasses

1 Water Jug with Initials J H K on a rais'd medallion

1 Pr Handsome Cut Butter Glasses (?) at Present Promis'd by Jac

do my Dear Davy let us have it before the 24 or really we must buy
some in town & dont forget the pretty little things I am very much
obliged for your sending the Cheese
I am going to write to my Dear Esther to ask her to come to town you
must try to Coax her but not for the World I dont want abrahams –
you can bring her I can make room for both of you ———————

The occasion for this letter was the first anniversary of Harriet Jacobs'
wedding to Jacob Keyser on 24th June 1807.[28] The recipient of the letter,
David Samuel, whom Harriet addresses familiarly as 'Punch', seems to
be in charge of the factory in Isaac's absence, or perhaps of the sales
department. In the letter Harriet sends news of her father's health,
implying that he is with her in London (she invites 'Dear Esther' to come
to town in her postscript): a trade card for the Keysers records them as
auctioneers at 13, New Bond Street.[29]

Not surprisingly, all the pieces mentioned by Harriet are table glass,
either from drinking or dessert services, intended for the anniversary
dinner.

Two items stand out immediately, the 'Blue & Gilt Edge Wine
Coolers' and blue and gilt edge 'finger Cups', items five and six. Glass
wine coolers, and indeed punch bowls, are mentioned in a sale catalogue
of 1823, part of the stock of a bankrupt glassmaker, John Honeybourne of
Kingswinford, near Stourbridge.[30] The finger cups probably refer to
what are now known as finger bowls, similar to the example illustrated as
plate 23.

As well as coloured glass, Harriet ordered cut glass, a combination of
drinking and dessert glass. The 'bonnet rummers' were larger glasses,
the shape probably dictating their name. 'Lemonades' appear again in
the Honeybourne bankruptcy sale catalogue of 1823.[31] According to
Robert Charleston, the examples of 1823 were probably similar to
Samuel Miller's drawings for the Waterford Glasshouse of 1830, and the
type merged eventually with the custard glass, which was probably
slightly smaller.[32] 'Jelly Glasses', the fourth item, were standard
components of the dessert service, which would probably also include
the stand listed as item one. The cut pieces would also probably include
item ten, the water jug, with its raised medallion probably engraved with
Harriet and Jacob's initials in monogram: the 'rais'd medallion' appears
to be an afterthought, being in a lighter script.

Two interesting points are made by the latter half of the list. Items
seven to nine are all to be made 'to match the last sent'. The current

enthusiasm for matching pieces and services has already been noted, but it was advertised as a particular attraction by Isaac in 1805:

> 'every attention paid to Articles sent to be made to pattern to complete imperfect Sets of Glass.'

The last item refers to an 18th century eating habit noted by the Duke of Rochefoucauld on a visit to England in 1784, brought to light by Robert Charleston.[33] When the cloth was drawn after dinner,

> 'On the middle of the table there is a small quantity of fruit, a few biscuits (to stimulate thirst) and some butter, for many English people take it as dessert.'

These items conclude the list of Harriet's requirements, which illustrate a range of highly fashionable glass from the Non-such Glasshouse.

It is fortunate that Harriet's note survived, and one may hope that her order arrived in time. It confirms that the Jacobs glasshouse could produce by 1808 glass in the latest fashion, a remarkable achievement from the modest beginnings of Lazarus, the immigrant glass-cutter in a highly competitive industry. It is doubtful whether the factory's cut glass products will ever be identified, yet it is still useful to be able to locate the glasshouse more precisely within the industry of its time, and to gain a more precise idea of its activities. Through the care of Harriet's descendants the City has also gained a valuable document to add to our knowledge of one of Bristol's best known glassmakers.

Notes

1. Catalogue of the Braikenridge Collection of Watercolours, a.34, City of Bristol Museum and Art Gallery: dated 'anno 1821'.

2. Letter from Harriet Keyser to David Samuel, June 10th, 1808, Bristol Record Office: see page 13.

3. Ex inf. W. S. Jessop, Franklin Lakes, New Jersey, U.S.A., 1971, quoted by Z. Josephs, 'The Jacobs of Bristol, Glassmakers to King George III', BGAS, v 95 1977, p 98.

4. Michael Edkins' Ledger 1761–86, p 44 (Bristol Reference Library B 20196).

5. Felix Farley's Bristol Journal, February 23rd, 1771.

6. Michael Edkins' Ledger 1761–86, p 89.

7. W. Barret, History of Bristol, 1789, p 556, quoted in Z. Josephs, op. cit., p 99.

8. Mathews' Directory for 1795.

9. Mathews' Directory for 1797.

10. Mathews' Directory for 1799–1800.

11. Felix Farley's Bristol Journal, April 20th, 1805.

12. Felix Farley's Bristol Journal, July 12th, 1806.

13. Billhead of Isaac Jacobs, City of Bristol Museum and Art Gallery, Mb 8764; see plate 14.

14. Z. Josephs, op. cit., p 100.

15. C. H. Walker, In the Matter of Jacobs, a Bankrupt (1821), Bristol Reference Library, B 1259, quoted Z. Josephs, op. cit., p 101. A purchaser from Baltimore of Jacobs' goods is documented for 1797 by Arlene Palmer Schwind in America and the Bristol Glass Trade, p 84 and note 29.

16. Ibid.

17. The note on glasshouses in the Braikenridge Collection catalogue (see note 1) includes the following in a list of glasshouses: 'Mr Isaac Jacobs, Flint & Cut Glass Manufacturer, Avon Street Great Gardens has just broken up his concern.'

18. See note 15.

19. Op. cit., p 10.

20. Op. cit., p 22.

21. Felix Farley's Bristol Journal, loc. cit.

22. See note 13.

23. Felix Farley's Bristol Journal, April 20th, 1805.

24. Michael Edkins' Ledger, loc. cit.

25. Op. cit., p 73.

26. Elisa Steenberg, Svensk Adertonhundratals Glas, Stockholm (1952), n.40, p 126, quoted by R. J. Charleston, 'A Glassmaker's Bankruptcy Sale', Transactions of the Glass Circle, Vol.2, pp 8–9.

27. See for instance the crested service of 56 dozen pieces ordered by William Greaves of Small Street, Bristol, for a Spanish client on February 15th, 1804 (Wedgwood Archive 6 – 10680): for further discussion, see Cleo Witt, 'Josiah Wedgwood and the Bristol Trade', Proceedings of the Twenty-sixth Annual Wedgwood Seminar, 1981, p 174 ff.

28. See transcript, page 13: two miniatures dated by tradition to 1807 are in the possession of descendants of Harriet and Jacob Keyser; they are half-length, and that of Jacob is signed 'T B'.

29. In the possession of descendants of Harriet and Jacob Keyser.

30. R. J. Charleston, op. cit., p 15, no.52, and p 14, no.64.

31. R. J. Charleston, op. cit., p 15, item 35. Lemonades of 'can' (that is cylindrical) shape were also among Bristol glass imported to America by William Rhinelander from Vigor and Stevens between 1773 and 1782: see Arlene Palmer Schwind, America and the Bristol Glass Trade, page 77.

32. R. J. Charleston, op. cit., p 9 and p 11, note 47.

33. (tr.) S. C. Roberts, A Frenchman in England in 1784, Cambridge (1933), p 30, quoted by R. J. Charleston, op. cit., p 9.

Plate 2.

A View of Totterdown by H. O'Neill. 1821.
Watercolour. Unsigned. M 2966. From the Braikenridge
Collection.
The three glasshouses in St. Philips dominate this view of
Bristol from the Bath approach: they are the Hoopers' and
Soapboilers' two glasshouses *(see pages 49–53)*, in Avon
Street and Cheese Lane.

Plate 3.

A View of St. Mary Redcliffe by H. O'Neill. c1821.
Watercolour. Unsigned. M3375. From the Braikenridge
Collection.
The Prewitt Street glasshouse which appears here still
survives as part of the Dragonara Hotel. Probably a late
18th century bottlehouse, it no longer functioned by 1812;
by the late 1930s, its upper brickwork showed cracks and
was demolished.
See page 55.

(Below) **A View of Glasshouses in St. Philips** by H.
O'Neill. c1821.
Watercolour. Unsigned. M2777. From the Braikenridge
Collection.
The two glasshouses on the left represent the Soapboilers
glasshouse in Cheese Lane, that on the right the Hoopers
glasshouse, which amalgamated with the Soapboilers
glasshouse in 1853. These were the last remaining
glasshouses in Bristol by the late 19th century.
See page 49.

Plate 4.

**Detail from AN EXACT
DELINEATION OF THE
FAMOUS CITTY OF
BRISTOLL AND SUBURBS,**
published by James Millerd,
c1710. M4173.
All except one of the six
glasshouses shown have brick-
built cones, the exception being
Redcliff Backs, showing the
earlier form, and then worked by
Thomas Ewen. Richard Warren
worked St. Thomas Street and
Redcliff Gate glasshouses, the
Perrott family, Red Lane, and
Temple Backs was worked by its
probable builders, the Bradley
family. The St. Philips
glasshouse across the river,
Coldharbour, later became Avon
Street glasshouse, and was built
c1708–10 by Abraham Elton.

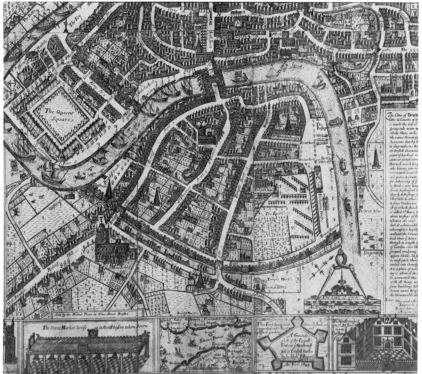

Plate 6.

Plate 5.

The Hotwell Glasshouse, anonymous. c1790.
Watercolour. Unsigned. M5245. From the Braikenridge
Collection.
The Limekiln Lane bottle house was close to the Hotwells
and to Jacob's Well, whose medicinal waters were bottled

and frequently exported from the early 18th century. This
view from the north west shows the rural setting of
startling contrast to the glasshouse, a feature also marked
in another view of thirty years later *(see plate 1).*
See page 53.

Plate 7.

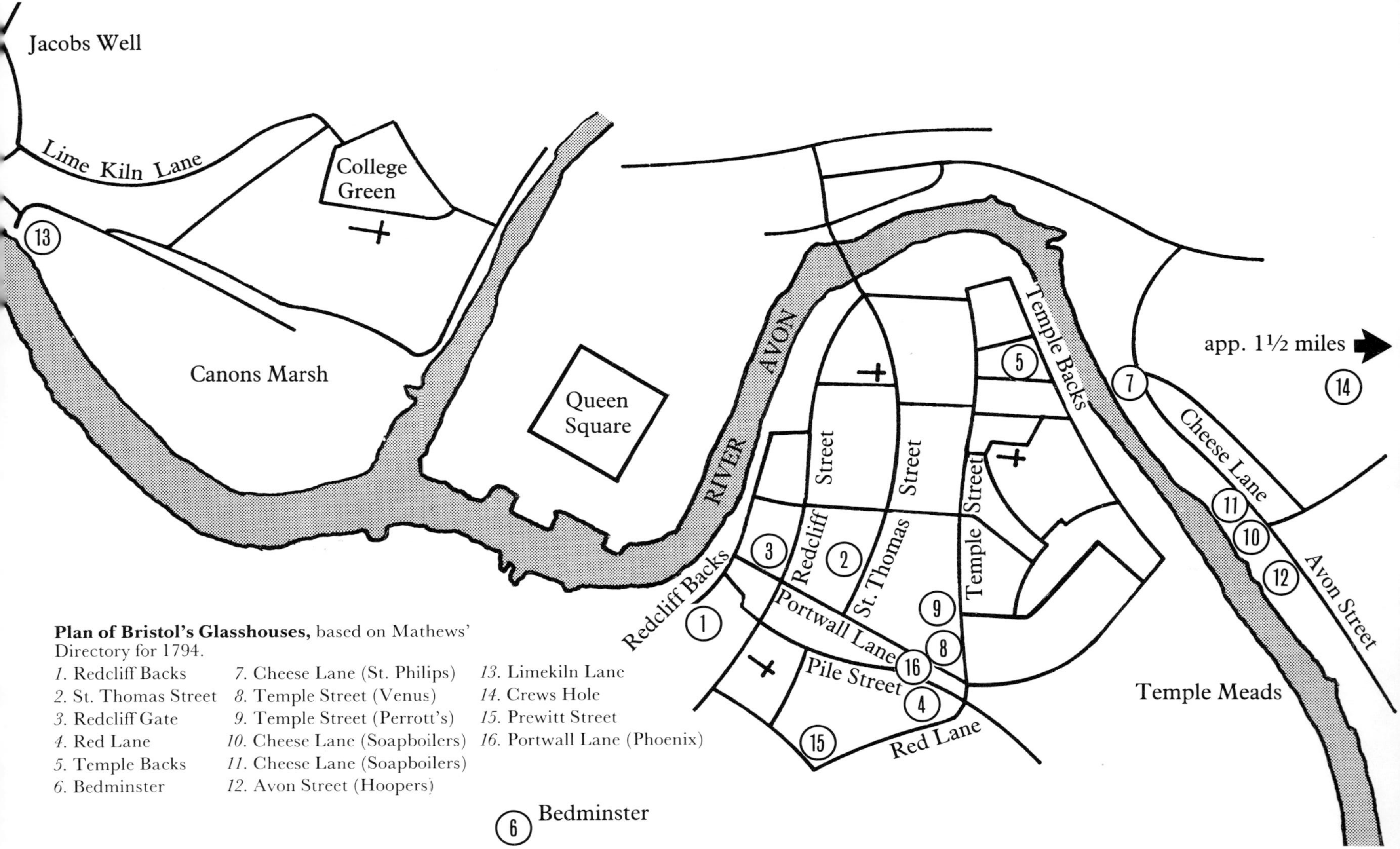

Jacobs Well

Lime Kiln Lane

College Green

Canons Marsh

Queen Square

RIVER AVON

Redcliff Backs

Temple Backs

Temple Street

St. Thomas Street

Redcliff Street

Redcliff Street

Portwall Lane

Pile Street

Red Lane

Cheese Lane

Avon Street

Temple Meads

app. 1½ miles

Bedminster

Plan of Bristol's Glasshouses, based on Mathews'
Directory for 1794.

1. Redcliff Backs
2. St. Thomas Street
3. Redcliff Gate
4. Red Lane
5. Temple Backs
6. Bedminster
7. Cheese Lane (St. Philips)
8. Temple Street (Venus)
9. Temple Street (Perrott's)
10. Cheese Lane (Soapboilers)
11. Cheese Lane (Soapboilers)
12. Avon Street (Hoopers)
13. Limekiln Lane
14. Crews Hole
15. Prewitt Street
16. Portwall Lane (Phoenix)

THE BRISTOL GLASSMAKERS

Early days

IN 1651 the iron masters in the Forest of Dean, faced with problems in making the pots in which they smelted their ore, called in 'an Ingenious Glass-Maker, Master Edward Dagney, an Italian then living in Bristow'. Dagney was probably one of the Dagnia family, brought to England by Sir Robert Mansell who, in the first half of the seventeenth century, held a monopoly in glassmaking. The Dagnia family did not continue working in Bristol, and Edward's sons, Onesiphorous, John and Edward, moved first to the glassmaking area of Stourbridge, and then to Tyneside.

There are earlier references to glassworkers in Bristol, in the late thirteenth and early fourteenth centuries, for example, but with no precise indication of the nature of their trade. Glaziers feature in the sixteenth century apprentices books, which is not surprising, since the demand for window glass for ecclesiastical use and, when the standard of living improved, for domestic purposes, was one of the main stimulants of the early native glass industry.

It was at the turn of the seventeenth century, however, that definitive evidence of the size and nature of the Bristol glass industry appeared. In 1696 John Houghton, in one of his letters on husbandry and trade, listed the glass houses in England and Wales. He recorded that 'In and about Bristol' there were five making bottles, one making bottles and window glass, and three making flint* glass and ordinary* glass. It was, outside London, the largest concentration of glasshouses.

Why Bristol?

What had attracted the glassmakers to Bristol? Until the first part of the seventeenth century glassmakers used wood to fire the furnaces in which they melted their glass. In 1615, however, in the face of an increasing demand for a decreasing commodity, the use of wood was forbidden to several industries, including that of glassmaking. The development of coal fired furnaces had already begun, and glassmakers started to move from the forests to those areas where coal was readily available. One such area was Bristol, but for the glassmakers it had additional attractions.

*In this context the term *flint* refers to lead glass, and the term *ordinary* to soda lime glass, on both of which there is further comment later. The products made from these glasses would be those mainly used for domestic purposes, for example, drinking glasses.

By the seventeenth century Bristol was already an established trading centre. As early as 1552 its merchants, in recognition of their success in developing foreign trade, had been incorporated as Merchant Venturers, under a charter granted by Edward VI. They had, by reason of their mercantile success, built Bristol into one of the most prosperous cities in the land. By the third quarter of the seventeenth century ships were sailing to New England, Virginia, Portugal, Spain and the northern European countries, carrying window glass and 'English glass bottles'.

Another factor was the availability of raw materials for making glass. Sand, limestone and red lead were available locally, or could if necessary be brought in by boat, as were special sands later. Kelp, subsequently burned, and in the form of ashes used as a flux for glass melting, was already imported from Ireland for soap making. Clay for making the pots in which the glass was melted could be shipped down the Severn from Stourbridge.

There was a further important factor. The importation of sugar, which was to become one of the commodities on which the fortunes of Bristol depended, led to a growth in liquor distilling. This, together with the traditional trade in wine and the locally produced beer and cider, provided markets for the glass bottle manufacturers.

The first set back

In 1695, faced with the need to pay for the war with France, the Government introduced an excise tax which, for the glass industry, was levied at 20% *ad valorem* on flint glass, 10% on window glass, and one shilling a dozen on bottles. The ultimate effect upon Bristol trade does not appear to have been too serious, but this may have been at the expense of neighbouring glassmakers. One of the Gloucester bottlemakers, for instance, in evidence to the House of Commons in February 1697, said that there were five glasshouses in Gloucester and Newnham and that not one of them had worked a fortnight since the duty commenced. Only one of the Gloucester glasshouses, and neither of the two at Newnham, went back into production, and it is likely that the Bristol bottle makers suffered temporary hardship since the increase in the price of bottles caused many of their customers to turn to casks.

Recovery with problems

The excise tax was repealed in 1699, and this appears to have stimulated the glass trade. Within the next quarter of a century a further five glasshouses were built, and Bristol was firmly established as an important centre of glassmaking. The expansion no doubt was encouraged by the confidence of the merchants. Daniel Defoe, visiting the city in the 1720s, commended their industriousness. Bristol was, he said, '. . . the greatest, the richest, and the best port of trade in Great Britain, London only excepted . . .'.

At the turn of the century the Bristol surveyor, James Millerd, published a series of maps of the city. On one version, that of *circa* 1710, the sites of six glasshouses are shown. The map is interesting in that each glasshouse, with one exception, is shown having a brick cone shaped chimney, a design of building that was to become universally used by glassmakers throughout the country. The cones were circular in cross section, on average about fifty feet in diameter at the base, rising to a height of one hundred feet, and sometimes more. When first introduced they could be unstable, as is instanced by the reports of those which fell down. In 1725 one collapsed in Bristol during a hurricane, with the loss of fourteen lives.

The design of the cones developed from the change from wood to coal fired furnaces, the cone providing both the extra draught required from the use of coal, and the means by which the noxious fumes were extracted from the working area. This was advantageous for the glassmakers, if not for the public in general, and led the Master of the Bristol Grammar School to comment on the pollution in no uncertain terms.

> 'Thick dark'ning Clouds in curling smoaky Wreaths
> Whose sooty stench the Earth and Air annoys
> And Nature's blooming Verdure half destroys.'

Since, according to Seyer, it was in 1698 or 1699 that the first brick building was erected in the city it must have been about the turn of the century that glasshouse cones began to appear on the Bristol scene.

But the smoke from the cones, and the danger of their collapsing, were not the only environmental problems set by the glassmakers. In 1700 the Corporation was empowered to fine glassmakers, among others, for throwing refuse into the river which was used universally as a tip. In the same year a committee was set up to 'examine into the case of strangers and all other disorderly persons' who came to live in the city, in order that they should not become chargeable to the parishes. The committee was enjoined to take particular care 'about workmen belonging to the glasshouses', which indicates a migration to Bristol at this time.

23

The early glasshouses

One site on the Millerd map, that by Redcliff Hill marked 'Glasshouse', has the appearance of the traditional wooden building that preceded the brick cone, and it was here that flint glass was made. The glasshouses at Redcliff Gate and St Thomas Street were owned by Richard Warren who, in an advertisement in 1712, offered crown** glass and bottles. The glasshouse in Red Lane was in the hands of the Perrott family, broad*** glassmakers who had migrated from Belbroughton to Bristol in the late seventeenth century, and who later changed to the manufacture of crown glass as a result of an agreement with the Stourbridge manufacturers. Bottles were made at the glasshouse on Temple Backs. Abraham Elton built the glasshouse on what is referred to as Coldharbour, and which later became Cheese Lane, and this was an interest that was to remain in the hands of various members of the family for the next century. Crown glass was made here. Finally, although not shown on the Millerd map, there was a flint glasshouse at Bedminster.

The merchants take an interest

Apart from the repeal of the excise tax, other developments in this period stimulated the growth of the glass industry in Bristol. Bath was moving toward its great period as a watering place, and needed window glass for its buildings, wine glasses for the dining tables, and bottles for drinks, both medicinal and alcoholic. Unfortunately, roads were bad and scarcely capable of taking the commercial traffic that Bristol was generating, let alone so fragile a commodity as glass. In his Builders Dictionary in 1726 Richard Neve wrote on the subject of window glass made in Bristol, '. . . but by reason they have not the Convenience to send it by Sea, . . . it is very rare to have any of it in London, tho' it be as cheap, and better than Newcastle Glass'.

In 1712, however, a plan for deepening and widening the Avon was drawn up and, by 1727, it was navigable to Bath. The route opened up a profitable business for the Bristol traders, and was probably the reason for the concentration of new glasshouses on the side of the Avon, in Cheese Lane and Avon Street. There was, however, another attraction in

Crown glass was window glass made by blowing a large sphere, then cutting it so that when rotated at speed it spread into a flat disc, which was later cut into the required sizes.

***Broad** glass was window glass made by elongating a sphere of glass into a sausage shape. The hemispherical ends were cut off and the resultant cylinder split down its length and flattened, before being cut to the sizes required.

the scheme to link the Avon to the Thames, and thus create a direct link between the two great ports of Bristol and London. So much so that in 1720 it was reported that several eminent merchants and tradesmen in the two cities had formed a co-partnership for the manufacture of glass.

By now the interest of the merchants had become a feature of the Bristol glass industry. In 1713, on the corner of Temple Street and Portwall Lane, a flint glasshouse known as the 'Venus' was built. There is reason for believing that the adjoining glasshouse, built at about the same time, belonged to Humphrey Perrott whose father, Benjamin, was the owner of the Red Lane glasshouse. In 1715 a group of soap boilers built a bottle glasshouse in Cheese Lane, and followed this some years later with a crown glasshouse on an adjoining site. Next to these, in 1720, Robert Hiscox, a barber surgeon, built a bottle glasshouse which, since five of the partners were hoopers, was subsequently known by that name. Away from this complex, on the west side of Canons Marsh, was another bottle glasshouse, well situated on the bank of the Avon and close to Hotwell and Jacob's Well, the waters of which were bottled and exported in substantial quantities.

By 1720, therefore, there were at least twelve glasshouses in Bristol, thus doubling the number shown on Millerd's map. Warren's glasshouse at Redcliff Gate was pulled down in 1718 to allow better access to Redcliff Backs, and the wooden building of the glasshouse on Redcliff Hill appears to have been replaced by a brick cone. The glass industry in Bristol was now well established, and only three more glasshouses were to be built within the boundary of the city, although subsequently some Bristol glassmakers were to extend their interests to Stanton Drew, Nailsea and Chepstow, with varying degrees of success.

The effect of peace and war

One of the contributory reasons for the successful growth of Bristol trade, and hence the growth of the glass industry, was the political stability of the country under Walpole. The war with France ended in 1713, and the subsequent financial and economic policies of the government aided industrial and commercial growth. But these policies were not without their problems. An attack was made on the evasion of customs duties, and a ban on the importation of wine in bottles was one way in which the glass industry was affected. However, when an attempt was made to introduce bonded warehouses for wine and tobacco the proposals met with strong opposition and had to be abandoned. Furthermore, the attempt to stem the increase in alcoholism by prohibitive taxation was openly defied, and whilst 'drunk for a penny, dead drunk for two pence' may have stimulated the sale of glass bottles, it did nothing to raise the confidence of the public in effective taxation.

Eventually the years of peace came to an end, and once again the Government was faced with the need to raise money for war. In 1745 the glass industry found itself again saddled with a tax which, half a century earlier, it had successfully appealed against. This time the protestations were not as successful, and it was a hundred years before the burden was lifted.

The glassmakers

Glassmaking in the eighteenth century had remained virtually unchanged for almost two thousand years, and its methods are similar to those used today when glass is made by hand. It has never failed to capture the imagination and those who queue today to see glass made this way were matched by their forebears in Bristol. Shiercliff, in his 1789 *Bristol and Hotwell Guide*, wrote, '. . . and to those who have never seen the manner of working this material, it may be a pleasing entertainment to attend the process . . . strangers are never denied seeing the people at work, on a small gratuity being given to the men employed'.

Glassmakers have always been proud of their skills. So confident, in fact, they are prepared to try their hand at making anything in glass. When the Prince and Princess of Wales visited Bristol in 1738 the report read as follows:

> 'The Company of Glassmen went first dressed in white Holland shirts, on horseback, some with swords, others with crowns and sceptres in their hands made of glass.'

These pieces, known as friggers, were usually made during break time, or at the end of the day, from glass at the bottom of the pot, and it was one of the ways in which the glassmaker improved his skills, and frequently his pocket, since they were often sold outside the glasshouse as mementos.

Not all commentators saw the glassmakers in so romantic a light. Patty More, visiting the Nailsea glasshouses with her sister toward the end of the eighteenth century was less than flattering when she wrote:

> 'The work of a glass-house is an irregular thing, uncertain whether by day or by night; not only infringing upon man's rest, but constantly intruding upon the privileges of the Sabbath. The wages high, the

eating and drinking luxurious – the body scarcely covered, but fed with
dainties of a shameful description. The high buildings of the glasshouses ranged before the doors of these cottages – the great furnaces
roaring – the swearing, eating, and drinking of these half-dressed,
black-looking beings, gave it a most infernal and horrible appearance.'

The wages of glassmakers appear to have been good, and although there
is not a great deal of comparative data, the principal glassmakers at the
Hoopers glasshouse in 1768, for instance, were earning between 3s. 9½d.
and 4s. a day, as against 2s. a day for building craftsmen.

A reputation is established

Whilst window glass, and in particular bottles, formed the basis of the
Bristol glass industry, its reputation was established by the flint
glassmakers. In 1675 glass with a high lead oxide content, 'glass of lead'
as it was termed, was introduced. Because of the ease with which it could
be worked, its clarity and quality, this glass soon began to replace the
conventional soda based flint glass. By the end of the seventeenth
century most, if not all, of the Bristol glasshouses that made domestic
products such as drinking glasses had adopted the lead glass.

It was, however, the second half of the eighteenth century that saw the
name of Bristol written into the history books on glass. It was during this
period that coloured glasses became popular, particularly blue glass,
subsequently associated with the expression 'Bristol blue'. Blue glass
was neither confined to this period, nor was it exclusive to Bristol, since
the use of cobalt as the means of obtaining this colour had been known to
glassmakers for centuries. It was, however, cobalt from a particular
source in Saxony which, in the eighteenth century, was credited with a
quality of colour that had never been surpassed. During the third quarter
of the century the British supply of cobalt from that source appears to
have been in the hands of William Cookworthy, a west country porcelain
manufacturer and raw materials merchant, who had built up
considerable interests in Bristol. Since Cookworthy imposed no
restrictions as to who could purchase from his stock of cobalt it was
readily available to glassmakers throughout the country. Thus, the term
'Bristol blue' could equally have arisen from the fact that Bristol was
where this colouring agent was purchased.

A further development in the second half of the eighteenth century was
that of opaque white glass, which resembled porcelain, but cost far less.
Widely made throughout the country, the quality of the product was

enhanced by decorators who painted flowers, birds, chinese and other motifs on the surface. Foremost among these was Michael Edkins, who began his career at the Bristol delftware works at Redcliff. Michael Edkins set up on his own *circa* 1760, and decorated for the Redcliff Backs glasshouse, the short lived glasshouse of William Dunbar and Co at Chepstow, and for the Bristol glass merchant, Lazarus Jacobs. Owing to the small amount being made at the time opaque white glass was not included in the 1745 excise act. This omission was rectified in 1778, when it was listed with flint glass, the rate of which that year was doubled, effectively killing the trade in opaque white glass.

The start of the decline

Any hope that the excise tax would quickly be withdrawn was dashed when, in 1756, war was declared on France. Worse was to follow from the government's policy toward the American colonies. Friction between the two sides led eventually to a non-importation agreement on the part of some of the colonies. Nothing could have been calculated to hit the Bristol merchants harder, and in 1775, the Merchant Venturers petitioned Parliament. They cited the effect that certain of the earlier duties had had on trade in 'glass, paper and other articles'.

This trade had revived since these duties had been repealed, but other measures were causing uneasiness. They concluded with a reference to 'the many thousands of miserable subjects who by the total stop put to the export trade to America will be discharged from their manufactories for want of employment and must be reduced to great distress'.

However, despite the imposition of the excise tax, glass production in the United Kingdom had gradually increased until, at the outbreak of the American War of Independence in 1775, it was some 70% higher than it had been in 1745, when the tax was introduced. Nevertheless, within three years production fell by one-third, and it was to be a further ten years before the previous level was regained. Bristol glassmakers, dependent as they were on the American colonies for much of their trade, may well have suffered more severely since it was this decade that marked the start of the decline of Bristol as a centre of glassmaking. A number of glasshouses came up for sale as some of the well known merchants and glassmakers began to withdraw from the trade.

Since the rush of investment at the early part of the century only two more glasshouses had been built; one at Crews Hole and the other on the continuation of Red Lane, later to become Prewitt Street. Now, with the industry in decline, a glasshouse was built on the site of the Phoenix Inn, on Portwall Lane. The man behind this enterprise was Jacob Wilcox Ricketts, of the Bristol glassmaking entrepreneurs possibly the most implacable, whose other interests included tobacco and brewing. Within the next twenty years Ricketts was to bring together all the Bristol flint glasshouses, re-open a bottle glasshouse, and make a handsome profit. All this, whilst the glass industry in Bristol was shrinking to about a quarter of its previous size.

The causes of the decline

The causes of the decline are complex, arising partly from the problems that faced the country as a whole, and partly from those that were particular to Bristol. The end of the eighteenth century saw England once more at war with France, and by the time the dispute was settled the glass industry had suffered two serious recessions. The excise tax on flint glass was by now some ten times greater than at the outbreak of the War of Independence, whilst the tax on bottles was up by about three and a half times. It could be argued that Bristol, with its high proportion of exports, and the drawback that these attracted, would have suffered less than other glassmaking areas. But a high proportion of these exports went to America, and that was where the problem began. As early as the seventeenth century the American colonists had hoped to create their own industries and William Penn, with Bristol support, had aimed at establishing glasshouses in Pennsylvania for the manufacturing of bottles, drinking glasses and window glass. But the policy of the British Government was to treat the colonies as sources of raw materials and markets for finished goods. The intention of the colonists was clear, and in 1771 the *Bristol Journal* carried a report of a meeting in Philadelphia where 'were exhibited several specimens of Flint Glass . . . Decanters, Wine Glasses, Beer Glasses, etc., manufactured by Mr Henry Stiegel, of Lancaster County, which were judged equal in beauty and quality to the generality of Flint Glass imported from England'.

Up to independence the American economy had developed fitfully. Once achieved, however, there was pressure for protection of the new and developing industries. In 1789 a duty was imposed on all imported glassware. The puff of cotton wool on the western horizon was beginning to turn into a storm cloud. Over the next few years these duties were gradually increased until, during the Anglo American war, they were doubled. But prior to this the English bottle makers had received a severe body blow. Under the existing tariff imported empty bottles were subject to a 10% *ad valorem* tax and, as a result, a good trade developed in re-using bottles which had been imported filled with liquor of one sort or another. The result was that in 1795 all imported bottles, whether empty or filled, were taxed at the same rate, with the result that British traders reverted to the policy of a century earlier and put their liquor into casks. The reason for so comprehensive a tariff structure was understandable, but in practice the American glassmakers could not meet home demand, as was shown by the massive increase in imports when the war came to an end. This was no consolation to the Bristol glassmakers since, by the time the markets reopened, most of their glasshouses were closed. Moreover, America was no longer the protected market of the British trader. Importers were free to buy in the cheapest market, and there were other glass industries in Europe anxious to exploit these opportunities.

In Bristol trade was controlled from the centre of the city, from which there was direct access to the sea. As one writer put it, '. . . in the middle of the street, as far as you can see, hundreds of ships, their masts as thick as they can stand by one another . . .'. But to get to the quays the Avon gorge had to be negotiated, and this involved additional expense since the ships had either to be towed, or the goods unloaded on to lighters. Furthermore the Avon was tidal, with a difference in levels greater than any other navigable river in western Europe, with the result that at low tide ships were reduced to lying on their side incapable of being loaded or unloaded. The situation called for a tideless basin, but prevarication delayed such a project for a century or more; by the time it was completed the relative importance of Bristol as a port had waned.

There were other problems associated with the docks, particularly those related to charges which, it was said,,were higher than those levied at Liverpool or London. Furthermore, the great dream of a direct river route to London by linking the Avon to the Thames, which may well have inspired some of the eighteenth century merchants to invest in the glass industry, was eventually realised some two hundred years after the idea was first mooted. Both this, and the floating harbour, however, were too late to be of great interest to the glass industry since, by the time the facilities became available in the early nineteenth century, only four of the sixteen glasshouses remained at work.

No reprieve

In 1820 the production of flint glass and bottles in the United Kingdom fell precipitously. The successful Phoenix glasshouse began to lose heavily and was never to regain its previous profitability whilst the decorating firm of Lazarus Jacobs, described in an advertisement as 'glass manufacturer to His Majesty', and for whom Michael Edkins had worked as early as 1763, went out of business.

On the previous occasion that an excise tax had been imposed the Bristol glassmakers had voiced their objections, but on this occasion they were less vociferous. By the time the Government set up an enquiry into its effect the Limekiln Lane bottle house was on the point of closing down, the Ricketts family seem to have lost their enthusiasm, and it was left to William Powell, proprietor of the Hoopers glasshouse in Avon Street, to present the Bristol point of view.

The report of the Commissioners, when it was published in 1835, was particularly revealing. It listed 106 glasshouses in England and 10 in Scotland. Most glasshouses were by now in the midlands and the north, with the north east, with 41 glasshouses, the predominate area. Bristol with four glasshouses, Nailsea with two and London with three were the only areas in the south where glassmaking continued. Just under 10% of all bottles, less that 3% of flint glass and no crown glass was now made at Bristol. Glassmaking had moved inexorably to those regions where coal was more readily obtained, and where the growing industrial towns had better means of communicating with their markets.

Plate 9.

A South East Prospect of Bristol, published by Buck. c1734. M 5289.

This panoramic view gives an even clearer impression of the contrast between the industrialised city centre and the surrounding upland, the St. Philips group to the right and the Temple Street group at the centre being particularly noticeable.

Detail from Rocque's MAP OF BRISTOL, published and sold by Benjamin Hickey, March 1743. M 768.

By 1743, Redcliff Gate glasshouse had been demolished (in 1710) to improve access from Redcliff Street to Redcliff Backs, and five other houses built. In Temple parish, the Venus glasshouse appeared in about 1713, producing flint glass until c1791, and from c1711 Humphrey Perrott, the son of a glassmaker, produced crown glass at the Temple Street glasshouse, the business ceasing between the 1760s and the end of the century. A consortium formed the Hoopers glasshouse in St. Philips, c1720, for bottle-making, and from c1715 a similar consortium of soap-boilers built adjacent crown and bottlehouses in Cheese Lane. Both became part of the Powell and Ricketts group eventually.

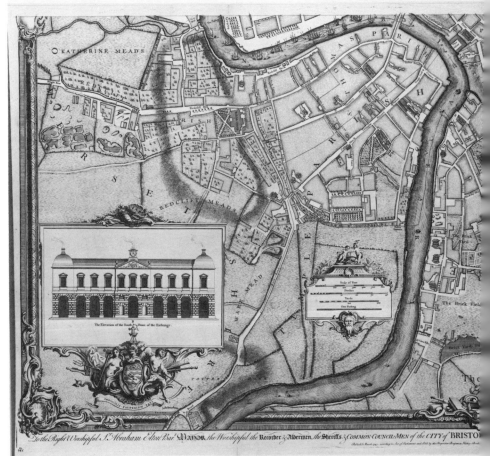

Plate 8.

A View of Redcliffe Church and Glassworks from the docks by George Cumberland. c1820.
Watercolour. Unsigned. From the Collection of Mrs. Joanna Lazarus.
The glasshouse illustrated is Redcliff Backs, which lay between St. Mary Redcliffe and the River Avon, and was a flint glasshouse. It appears on Millerd's map of 1710, but seems by 1820 to have closed down.
See page 35.

Plate 11.

(Below) **A View of Bristol from Ashton Park** by Samuel Colman. c1822.
Oil on canvas. Signed 'S. Colman'. K 4350.
Bristol's industrial townscape viewed from the rural setting of the further bank of the River Avon.

Plate 10.

Plate 12.

(Above) **Inside a glass house on the Hotwells Road,** by George Cumberland. c1820.
Watercolour. Unsigned. From the Collection of Mrs. Joanna Lazarus.
A leaf from the Bristol artist's sketchbook, presenting a vivid impression of the interior of the Limekiln Lane glasshouse; against the wall appear to lean blowing irons, while between the furnace and the seated men are probably the marvering surface and the mould for bottles. *See page 53.*

(Below) **Detail from the Coronation Procession for William IV,** published by William Greethead, 1831.
Watercolour on paper. Mb 846.
This group of glassmakers formed part of the Bristol Coronation procession, bearing spectacular examples of their craft. In 1738 the Prince and Princess of Wales were greeted by a procession in which the Company of Glassmen went on horseback, "some with swords, others with crowns and sceptres in their hands made of glass." (*Daily Post,* November 14 1738, quoted A. C. Powell, *Glassmaking in Bristol,* Transactions of the Bristol and Gloucestershire Archaeological Society, 1925, p. 218.)

Plate 13.

Carpenters   *Glass workers*   *Pipe makers*   *Brick makers*

THE BRISTOL GLASSHOUSES

1. Redcliff Backs

ON THE Millerd map of 1710 this glasshouse is positioned outside the city wall, between Redcliff Hill and the River Avon, on a site known as Redcliff Pitt. The building shown on the map was replaced by a brick cone, and later referred to as the Redcliff Backs glasshouse. It could be conjectured that this was the glasshouse at which the Dagnia family worked in the mid 17th century. However, there is evidence that associates this glasshouse with the Lowden family, of which John Lowden in 1673 was the first glassmaker to appear in the Burgess Books as a freeman, and over the next century several members of the family were either bound apprentices to glassmakers, or had apprentices bound to them. Although it is not clear whether they continued to work at this glasshouse, many of them are believed to have done so.

From 1700 to 1710 apprentices were bound to Thomas Ewens, and the glasshouse seems to have been under his ownership until 1717. Subsequently, Captain Wheeler ran it from 1721 to 1723, John Jones from 1724 to 1740, and then his widow until 1746. The glasshouse appears to have been unused until 1750, when it came into the hands of Crosse and Berrow who, according to the notice when they took it over, made 'the best flint and green glass'. It was they who, in 1752, when duty was charged on exported bottles as well as on the contents, brought an action against the Crown, and won. When they went bankrupt in 1760 the stock was described as 'the best white and flint wares', suggesting therefore that they had been making enamel glass. It is interesting to surmise that Michael Edkins, earlier employed by an adjacent pottery as a delftware painter, subsequently decorated glassware for Crosse and Berrow, since the demise of the glasshouse coincides with the generally accepted date at which he became an independent decorator. He subsequently worked for Little and Longman, who ran the glasshouse from 1761 to 1767. Robert Vigor joined the concern in 1767, and the name was changed to Longman and Vigor, but when Longman died the following year Vigor ran it alone until joined by Stevens. By 1775 it had become Vigor, Stevens and Hill, and in the same year the crown glasshouse in St Thomas Street became part of the concern. Robert Vigor was drowned in 1782, whilst watering his horse at a pond, and at this point, having made a profit of £16,140 over the previous fourteen years, the concern began to lose money, to the extent of £35,000 over the next fourteen. The imposition of an excise tax on enamel glass in 1778 no doubt caused problems, since it was from the following year that profits began to fall.

The glasshouse had its share of the limelight. In 1770, *Felix Farley's Bristol Journal* records that '. . . Le Prince de Pigniotelli and Le Chevalier de Tournelle, who are now making a Tour of this Kingdom . . .' came to Bristol and were taken to see Vigor and Stevens, whilst in 1781 a Joseph Baggs was convicted of robbing and setting fire to the 'accompting house'. Eight years later an acrimonious exchange took place publicly in the Bristol newspapers when two of their clerks left, one to join the Venus glasshouse, and the other the newly built Phoenix glasshouse. An employee from the St Thomas Street glasshouse was also involved in the defection.

For some years, despite the death of Robert Vigor, the name remained Vigor and Stevens, with the variation in 1789 of Vigor, Stevens, Randolph and Stevens. In 1793 it became Stevens, Randolph and Co, but this changed to Stevens, Cave and Co when John Cave and George Daubeny, Bristol merchants of some stature, joined William and James Stevens. Following a dispute in August of the same year, James Stevens left. William Stevens became a bankrupt in 1798 and his two partners took over the glasshouse and ran it, together with the glasshouse in St Thomas Street until 1802, when an amalgamation took place with Wadham Ricketts and Co, of Portwall Lane. Their intervention had been successful, as can be seen from the profits of the concern which from 1795 to 1800 totalled £3,420. Following the amalgamation both the Redcliff Backs and the St Thomas Street glasshouses closed down.

2. St Thomas Street

This glasshouse, shown on the Millerd map, is the subject of an advertisement in the *Post Man*, May 17th, 1712:

> 'At Mr Richard Warrens and Company's Glasshouse in St Thomas Street, Bristol are to be sold all sorts of very good Crown Glass, wholesale or retale; and at the same house are made all sorts of very good Bottles; all sold as cheap as at any place in England.'

Richard Warren owned another glasshouse at Redcliff Gate, also shown on the Millerd map.

The Warren family held this glasshouse for many years, and well into the second half of the eighteenth century there are records of apprentices bound to one or other of the family. In 1752 the concern is listed as

Thomas Warren and Co, when an accusation of stealing a brass mould valued at 18 shillings (90p), was made against a James Watkins, but he was later acquitted. Richard Warren died in 1767 and the following year Richard Cannington, Richard Reynolds and William Cowles, already involved in the Temple Street flint glass house and the Avon Street bottle glasshouse expanded their interests by taking over the concern, which by then was making solely crown glass.

Six years later, during a violent storm, the cone was blown down, '. . . which occasioned such a shock that the neighbours, who were in their Beds, were greatly alarmed, apprehending it to be an Earthquake . . .'. This report refers to '. . . an old Glass House, not used for some time . . .', which suggests that the new partnership had suspended production. Later that year it came on to the market, together with the '. . . Phoenix Glass House . . .'. Since the glasshouse that became popularly known by this name had yet to be built it is possible that this is a misquote and refers to the Temple Street flint glasshouse, known as the Venus, and owned by the same consortium. When ownership changed the same year the new agreement referred to '. . . a ruinous glass house built by Richard Warren . . . late in occupation of Messrs Marcus and Cannington and Co or their under tenants . . .'.

In 1775 ownership passed to Vigor and Stevens, who were making flint glass at Redcliff Backs, and the cone presumably was rebuilt. From then on the two glasshouses ran as one concern and remained so until the amalgamation with Wadham Ricketts and Co in 1802.

3. Redcliff Gate

This glasshouse, shown on the Millerd map *circa* 1710, was run by Richard Warren in conjunction with the St Thomas Street glasshouse, although Buckley suggests that previously it was in the hands of William Baron. It was, however, demolished around 1718 in order to give better access to Redcliff Backs from Redcliff Street. Since Richard Warren and Co made both crown glass and bottles, and since the St Thomas glasshouse was known later to specialise in the former, it is possible that this was a bottle house.

4. Red Lane

This glasshouse, shown on the Millerd map 1710, is known to have been in the hands of the Perrott family, and possibly built by them. The

Perrotts were broad glassmakers who migrated from Belbroughton to Bristol in the latter part of the seventeenth century. In 1692 John Perrott took Benjamin, the son of Benjamin Perrott, as an apprentice, and then from 1701 to 1738 there are records of Benjamin junior taking apprentices.

The Perrotts were involved in one of the earliest restrictive trading agreements when, in 1703, they agreed with the Stourbridge broad glass making families of Henzey, Tyzack and Batchelor, not to make any broad glass for eleven years except in London, or within ten miles of London Stone, which scarcely affected the agreement since their glasshouse was in Bristol. The Stourbridge glassmakers on their side agreed to deliver to the Perrotts annually, eight score cases of window glass. Should the price of window glass encourage others to start production, or should the delivery of the glass lapse, the agreement would be wound up and the Stourbridge glassmakers would supply sufficient workmen to the Perrotts to enable them to recommence production. Professor Court suggests that there is evidence that the practice worked for several years, but that by 1712 a price war had broken out. It could have been that the growing popularity of crown glass, which offered a superior if more expensive window glass, helped to break up the agreement. The Perrotts became crown glassmakers, and since they continued to make glass during the life of the agreement it must be assumed that this did not constitute a breach of the agreement. Benjamin Perrott senior was much concerned at the waste of glass that resulted from the breakage of the pots in which glass was melted. In 1720 he was granted a patent for inventing a means by which such occurrences would be prevented. By 1745 there are references to Benjamin Perrott the younger, suggesting that there was a third generation of glassmakers of the same name at work in Bristol.

In 1752, however, the glasshouse was let to Daniel Taylor on a 21 year lease at an annual rent of £125, but he died three years later. The glasshouse came up for sale and was taken over by the sons, Samuel and Daniel Taylor, who also seem to have been expanding their interests since Daniel Taylor bought land, including the Phoenix Inn, from the Perrott family. This property was to play an important role in Bristol glassmaking later in the century. An announcement in 1762 asked for information about an absconded employee, Thomas Holden, who had embezzled a considerable sum of money from the Taylors by forging their names. In 1783 the partnership, by then in the name James Taylor and Bros was dissolved, and the glasshouse came into the possession of

Plate 14.

Billhead of Isaac Jacobs, c1806–21.
Signed by the engraver 'Silvester, 17 Strand, London'.
Mb 8764.
From 1806, Jacobs described himself as 'Glass
Manufacturer to His Majesty'; the glass trade he carried
on is represented by the cones and sailing ships, from 1805
based at the 'Non-such Flint Glass Manufactory',

completed in that year. Both he and his father Lazarus are
more notable as decorators and suppliers than as
producers. Lazarus first appears as a "Glass Cutter",
while Isaac opened in 1805 "A New Set of Rooms on
purpose for the Retail Trade".
See page 10.

Plate 15.

**Detail of Wineglass Cooler and
Fragment of Decanter,** Isaac Jacobs,
c1805.
Blue glass with gilded signature 'I.
Jacobs/Bristol'. West Country Collection/
G3302. Ht. 9.6 cm.; diam. 9.5 cm.
See page 12.

'Hollands' Decanter and Stopper, Isaac Jacobs, c1805.   *Plate 16.*
Blue glass enriched with gilding: base signed in gold 'I. Jacobs/Bristol'. From a Private
Collection. Ht. 28 cm.
Probably one of a set in stand like the group illustrated in plate 21. The interlaced paterae on
the simulated label occur on a number of this type of decanter, typical of the attenuated neo-
classicism prevalent in the 1790s.
See page 12.

Plate 17.

(Above) **Billhead of Wadham Ricketts & Co.,** Phoenix Glasshouse. c1790.
Signed in print by the engraver 'Doddrell Sculpt'. MB3763.
The fashionably neo-classical surround for the glasshouse vignette was probably a standard motif, contrasting with the more diagrammatic drawing of the glasshouse itself. In style the decanters shown appear earlier than the 1790s, and may again have been a stock pattern from the previous quarter of the century.

(Left) **Saucebottle and Stopper,** Wadham Ricketts & Co., Phoenix Glasshouse, 1798. Blue glass enriched with gilding: base acid-etched 'W R & Co 1798'. N8001. Ht. 12 cm. Saucebottles took their form from decanters: their size and purpose derive from the taste for hot spicy sauces such as 'ketchup' or 'anchovy', brought back by travellers or residents from the East Indies.
See page 56.

Plate 18.

Plate 20.

(Above) **The 'Nugent' goblet,** probably Bristol, c1754.
Flint glass, tulip bowl on mixed twist stem: bowl wheel-engraved 'Health to the Honble. Robt. Nugent Esq.'
G 374. Ht. 19.1 cm.
Sir Robert Nugent was one of the two successful candidates at the Bristol parliamentary elections of 1754: the centre of a tinglazed earthenware plate in the City of Bristol Museum and Art Gallery bears the inscription 'Nugent Only' (G 1699).

(Left) **The 'Dreadnought' Privateer Glass,** probably Bristol, c1757.
Flint glass, wheel-engraved with a privateer and 'Success to the DREADNOUGHT Privateer', on a multi-ply opaque-twist stem. From the Collection of Mrs. Joanna Lazarus. Ht. 15.5 cm.
Two 'Dreadnought' privateers were commissioned, the earlier in 1745: the style of this glass suggests the later ship, which set sail under Captain James Leisman on March 22nd, 1757, during the Seven Years War (see Cdr. J. W. Damer Powell, *Bristol Privateers and Ships of War*, p 200 ff). *See also note (page 7) on jacket illustration.*
Plate 19.

Elton, Miles and Co, who already worked the crown glasshouse in Cheese Lane.

At this time the crown glass trade was beginning to recover after several years of depression, but whether Elton, Miles and Co took it over in order to increase their output or, alternatively, to close down competition, is not known. In the 1790s the newly built crown glasshouses at Nailsea would have posed a threat for the Bristol crown glassmakers, and in addition, Elton, Miles and Co had already complained that the Nailsea glasshouses had poached their workers.

In 1791 there was a proposal to develop the site, but doubt as to the legality of this prevented such action and the premises appear to have remained unworked until 1824, when William and Thomas Powell took them over and transferred their salt-glaze stoneware pottery from St Thomas Street to the site. In that year the Powells went into the glass bottle trade when they took over the glasshouse in Avon Street, known as the Hoopers. They also moved their glass cutting shop, for which they bought blanks from a glasshouse in Dudley, from Bath Parade to Red Lane, but withdrew from this trade soon after 1825 when the drawback on exports of flint glass was reduced. William Powell, in his evidence to the Commissioners of Inquiry into the excise tax, complained that this had meant 'the trade has not been worth a straw since'.

The cone was eventually pulled down in 1906 to make way for the development of the Mardon Son and Hall factory. Following destruction in 1940 it is now the site of the Mardon Caxton House.

5. Temple Backs

A. C. Powell credits the Bradley family with having built this glasshouse, which is shown on the Millerd map. Certainly this family owned the concern at some time prior to 1750, since that year it came on the market credited as being 'late in the possession of Robert Bradley and Co'. In 1795 Mathews *Bristol Directory* records James Jones as making 'black bottles' at Temple Backs, and also at Crews Hole. James Jones also took an interest in the Temple Street flint glasshouse when the partnership was reformed in 1789, and joined the Phoenix glasshouse when the two amalgamated. He died on March 21st, 1795, and it seems there were no buyers for the Temple Backs glasshouse when it came up for sale although, since it continued to be referred to in the directories until 1805, Thomas Jones may have continued to use the premises as a warehouse, if not as a manufactory, for some years.

6. Bedminster

'The hospital of St Catherine was in Bedminster where now a glasshouse is built.' So wrote Barrett in 1789, and this at least points to its site, although little is known about this glasshouse. By the early part of the nineteenth century the site had become a tan-yard and on the Ashmead map of 1833, is shown at the junction of East Street and Bedminster Parade. It was at one time associated with the Little family, and on July 11th, 1752, the *Bristol Journal* recorded that Mr Little 'proprietor of the white flint glasshouse at Bedminster', had died. It is possible that the Bedminster glasshouse went out of business in the late 1780s, since the UK glass trade as a whole suffered as a result of the American revolt and took some time to recover. The problems of the flint glass manufacturers were intensified by the swingeing tax on enamel glass in 1778 which may have affected Bedminster in the way that it seems to have affected the Redcliff Backs glasshouse.

7. Cheese Lane (St Philip's)

This glasshouse, built by Abraham Elton,* stood by the ferry which by 1841 was replaced by St Philip's bridge. It appears on the Millerd map 1710 on the bank of the Avon behind St Philip's church on land already owned by the family. By 1736 the glasshouse was well established since during that year the furnaces were down for re-building. Regrettably whilst the work was being carried out the glasshouse cone collapsed; '. . . happy it was for the Glass-men that the Fire was out, and only some few masons were employed in the repair of it . . .'. So read the report in the *General Advertiser*.

A. C. Powell suggests that it was managed by the Taylor family, basing this on the evidence that an apprentice of Sir Abraham Elton was turned over to Daniel Taylor in 1743. But in 1716 an apprentice of a Daniel Taylor was turned over to Richard Warren, as was his son Samuel Taylor the following year, which points at that time to an association with the St Thomas Street glasshouse. There is a specific

---

*It cannot be said with certainty which Abraham Elton founded this glasshouse and Lady Elton suggests it was a joint venture of the first and second baronets *circa* 1708–10. Theirs careers followed similar courses. Both became members of the Corporation of the City of Bristol, and in due course were both Sheriff and Mayor. Both became Master of the Merchant Venturers and represented Bristol in Parliament.

mention of 'my Crown works' in the will of the second Sir Abraham Elton and an association with the Taylor family who were specialists in this product would have been a sensible arrangement.

The second Sir Abraham Elton died in 1742, the year preceding that in which the apprentice was turned over to Daniel Taylor, which could mean that by now Taylor had moved from St Thomas Street to St Philip's, prior to taking over the Red Lane glasshouse in 1752. Daniel Taylor bought land in the area from the Elton family, and in 1771 a 'piece of ground' in Martin's Lane, adjoining the St Philip's glasshouse, and owned by the Taylors, came up for sale.

In 1746 the third Sir Abraham Elton was declared bankrupt, and it is possible that at this point the glasshouse was taken over by his cousin, Isaac Elton who was later to become partner in the adjacent soap boiler's glasshouses. In 1751, a notice for the auction of some houses refers to them as 'near Mr Elton's glasshouse', whereas previous notices referred to the glasshouse as that of Sir Abraham Elton.

Over the next half century there are further occasional references. On October 4th, 1755, it was reported that '. . . a man, being disordered in his senses, jumped into a pot of hot metal at a Glasshouse behind St Philip's . . .'. By the 1790s it appears to have operated as Elton, Miles and Co, and then a few years later as Elton, Miles and Wilcox, in conjunction with the two soap boilers glasshouses, which had been acquired by this consortium, and presumably it shut down when they ceased production *circa* 1810.

8. Temple Street (Venus)

On February 17th, 1713, an agreement was signed between John Cook, yeoman; Stephen Collier, glassmaker; Francis Ironntain, house carpenter; James Hilhouse, merchant; in which they became partners '. . . in the Art Trade or Mistory of making or selling Flint and Green Glass and other Glass wares in such a manner as they should think fitt . . .'. The agreement went on to refer to '. . . their Glasshouse Glassworks Warehouses and Buildings situate in Temple Street . . .'. Apprentices were indentured to Stephen Collier and John Cook, and the glasshouse was known as Collier Cook and Co until, in 1741, it changed to Francis Cook and Co.

In 1754 the partnership was re-formed, the previous partners having died. This time James Hilhouse, merchant and son of one of the initial partners, Richard Reynolds, ironmonger, whose son of the same name was to become closely associated with the Coalbrookdale iron works, and Richard Cannington, glassmaker, were each to have one quarter share, whilst Francis Cook and Thomas Serle, both glassmakers were to divide the remaining one quarter share on a two to one basis. Richard Cannington and Thomas Serle were to be full time 'Clerks, Riders of Journeys and Managers'. The concern was valued at £1,031. 6. 7., which the new partners increased to £2,000, and was to be known as Francis Cook and Co.

By 1765 Cornelius Fry, a friend of William Cookworthy who by then was supplying, among other raw materials, cobalt from Saxony for blue glass, had joined the partnership. By this time Richard Reynolds senior had retired to Bath, where he died in 1769; his son Richard had taken his place in the partnership and the glasshouse was now known as Cannington, Reynolds and Fry. In the 1770s both Richard Cannington and Thomas Cannington took apprentices.

With the flint glass trade in the doldrums in the 1780s, Richard Reynolds and his partners decided to withdraw leaving Richard Cannington as the proprietor. The glasshouse ran as Richard Cannington and Co from 1786 to 1789 and was then taken over by James Jones, who already had other glassmaking interests in the city, William Fry, a distiller but no relation to the previous partner with the same surname, and John Mayo Tandey, previously employed at the St Thomas Street glasshouse and party to the acrimonious and public quarrel with William Stevens. Richard Cannington was no longer a partner in the concern, and four years later he died. The family interest in glassmaking was to continue elsewhere, however, and can be traced to St Helens, Lancashire, and to the formation of United Glass Bottle Manufacturers Ltd.

The glasshouse ran as Fry, Jones, Tandey and Co for two years before amalgamating with Wadham, Ricketts and Co, who occupied a newly built glasshouse on a facing site in Portwall Lane. The Temple Street glasshouse was let to a partnership consisting of a woollen draper, a hatter and a grocer, presumably for purposes other than making glass, and flint glass production continued in Portwall Lane under the name Wadham, Fry, Ricketts and Co.

9. Temple Street (Perrott's)

Humphrey Perrott, the second of Benjamin Perrott's two glassmaking sons, was born in 1690, and in common with his brother Benjamin was apprenticed at the age of fourteen. By 1715 he was taking apprentices,

Plate 21.

Three Decanters and Stoppers in Stand, Isaac Jacobs, c1805.
Blue glass enriched with gildings: 'Brandy' and 'Rum' inscribed in gold on base 'I. Jacobs/Bristol'. Brandy ht. 22.6 cm.; Rum ht. 23.3 cm.; Hollands ht. 22 cm. NX 1128 a – d.
Mallet-shaped body and target-shaped stopper typical of the late 18th – early19th century; also typical is the spare, delicate gilding with simulated wine-label.
See page 12.

Plate 22.

Decanter Stand or Dish, Isaac Jacobs, c1805.
Blue glass enriched with gilding: base inscribed in gold 'I. Jacobs/Bristol'. N 2031. Diam. 19.6 cm.
Armorial of the Earls of Verulam: part of the highly lucrative trade in personally decorated pieces, also seen in creamware and porcelain. In 1806 Jacobs advertised in *Felix Farley's Bristol Journal* "Coats of Arms, Crests & Cyphers done upon (Dessert Sets) in the greatest style, by some of the Finest Artists in the Kingdom".
See page 12.

Plate 23.

Finger Bowl, Isaac Jacobs, c1805.
Blue glass enriched with gilding: base inscribed in gold 'I. Jacobs/Bristol'. N 8087. Ht. 8.2 cm.
Greek key pattern characteristic of the rich simplicity of the Greek Revival of the early 1800s. Perhaps to be identified with the 'Finger Cups' mentioned by Harriet Keyser in her letter of 1808.
See page 13.

Plate 24.

Wineglass Cooler, Isaac Jacobs, c1805.
Blue glass enriched with gildings: base inscribed in gold 'I. Jacobs/Bristol'. West Country Collection. Ht. 9.6 cm.
Two-lipped form which held the wine glass upside down while not in use, its bowl in water, its stem and foot extended above the rim. Perhaps to be identified with the 'Blue & Gilt Edge Wine Coolers' referred to by Harriet Keyser in her letter of 1808.
See pages 12 and 13.

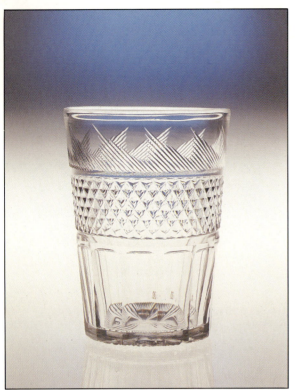

Plate 25.

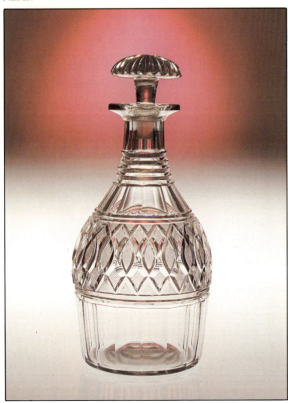

Plate 26.

(Left) **Tumbler,** W. & T. Powell, Red Lane Glasshouse, c1825–30.

Flint glass, wheel-cut. G 620. Ht. 12.1 cm. Given to the Museum and Art Gallery by A. C. Powell, partner in Powell & Ricketts 1889–1906, sole manager 1906–19, and Bristol glass historian. According to the inventory of the City Museum and Art Gallery, this piece was made and cut in Bristol: its strongly articulated decoration and deep cutting are typical of the 19th century's development of the art from the shallower reflective decoration of the mid 18th century.
See page 37.

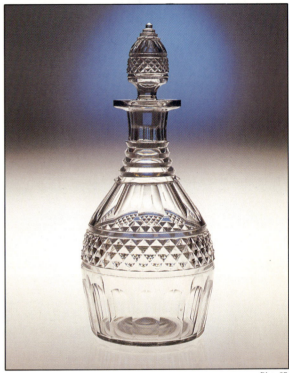

Plate 27.

(Above) **Decanter and stopper,** W. & T. Powell, Red Lane Glasshouse, c1825.

Flint glass, wheel-cut. G 602. Ht. 28 cm. Given by A. C. Powell: according to inventory, made by Badger's of Dudley and cut in Bristol.
A group of similarly shaped decanters is illustrated by Greethead in his *1831 Coronation Procession*, though only an outline and little detail can be seen.

(Left) **Decanter and stopper,** W. & T. Powell, Red Lane Glasshouse, c1825.

Flint glass, wheel-cut. G 601. Ht. 28 cm. Given by A. C. Powell: according to inventory, made by Badger's of Dudley and cut in Bristol.
Fine quality of cutting allies this to the other Powell examples, particularly the scentbottle G 625, which shares the fine double-cutting. Typical of this style is the sharply articulated pattern of cutting (compare the jug painted by Rolinda Sharples illustrated in *Study of Flowers*, K 1086).

and continued to do so until 1729, at least. Humphrey Perrott, like his father, was interested in technical matters and in 1734 took out a patent for a furnace which, it was claimed, would reduce the cost of melting glass. Unfortunately, in 1730, he had been declared bankrupt. However, it was not until 1744 that a notice appeared in the Bristol papers advertising for sale, '. . . The Dwelling house, together with several other Messuages, Glass Houses and other edifices with appurtenances late of Humphrey Perrott, a Bankrupt, situate lying and being in and near Temple Street, in Bristol . . .'. This suggests that he was allowed to continue as a glassmaker although a bankrupt, possibly on the strength of the returns from his patent.

Humphrey Perrott was a crown glassmaker, as was his father and brother. It would seem, therefore, that whilst his brother took over the family crown glasshouse in Red Lane, Humphrey Perrott built or took on the second of the two Temple Street glasshouses sometime between 1711, when he would have been qualified to become a freeman, and 1715, when he is recorded as having taken an apprentice. A further notice in 1766, and again ten years later, offers the glasshouse 'formerly in the possession of Humphrey Perrott' for sale by auction, 'on a yearly chief rent of 20s', but it does not appear to have been taken. A. C. Powell suggests that it was later used as a stocking factory, but Buckley, on the strength of an advertisement in 1798 which refers to '. . . that capital Crown and Flint Glass Manufactory situate in Portwall Lane and St Thomas Street . . . lately worked by Messrs Stevens, Cave and Company . . .', is of the view that it could have been absorbed into the Vigor and Stevens partnership. It is more likely that the advertisement should have referred to Redcliff Backs rather than Portwall Lane.

10. & 11. Cheese Lane (Soap Boilers)

Soap making was one of the earliest of the industries associated with Bristol, having been introduced initially to serve the woollen industry. After a recession due to Charles I's granting a trading monopoly to London, the trade once again became active in the eighteenth century. One problem the soap makers had was the disposal of the residues of their processes. The fats were treated with a caustic alkali, obtained by boiling lime with plant ash; the subsequent reaction precipitated calcium carbonate, known as soapers ash, the disposal of which became an environmental hazard. As early as 1621 an enactment forbade any person to '. . . cast or lay . . . any soap ashes, either in the river or within one hundred foot of full sea . . .'. Calcium carbonate can be used for making glass, and the growing market for bottles and window glass gave the soap boilers an opportunity of turning their waste material to use. In 1715 Edmund Mountjoy, later to become Sheriff and then Mayor of Bristol, John Purcell, John Thomas and Elisha Hellier, all of them in the business of soap making, built a bottle glasshouse in Cheese Lane, and a few years later, a crown glasshouse on an adjoining site.

In 1751, the *Bristol Weekly Intelligencer* carried a reference to the sale of '. . . Three houses opposite Mr Tyndall's first glasshouse . . .' and this revised ownership is confirmed in a deed two years later which refers to Thomas Tyndall, Onesiphorous Tyndall, Corsley Rogers, a merchant; Arthur Jepson, a wine merchant; William Hall, a dry-salter; and William King, a glassmaker; as '. . . co-partners in the undertaking of making glass bottles and other glassware . . .'. Thomas Tyndall was a Bristol business man of some standing, and the partnership was an example of the way in which financial and marketing interests in Bristol combined with manufacturing skills.

Over the next few years the partnership appears to have changed since, on August 16th, 1766, a notice appeared in the *Bristol Journal* announcing the dissolution of a partnership between William King and Thomas Harris, and this was followed some seven weeks later by a further announcement that the equipment of the two glasshouses in Cheese Lane, together with that of a third at Crews Hole, would be auctioned, as would one-third of the share in the glasshouses, for the remainder of their leases. There was a lack of harmony in this affair: James Allcott, described as a co-assignee in the premises, announced that he did not agree with the sale. Later that year the glasshouses came under the control of John Coghlan, Samuel Peach, his son-in-law Isaac Elton, William Miles and Matthew Cowper, and thus associated with the St Philip's glasshouse. At first it appears to have been known as Peach, Coghlan and Co, but when both Peach and Coghlan had died in the mid 1780s it became Elton, Miles and Co, as was the St Philips glasshouse at the time.

By 1793 the partners were William Miles, Robert Hurst, John Wilcox and Isaac Elton junior, and their ownership had been extended to include the Red Lane glasshouse. In 1799 John Wilcox took over Robert Hurst's share, and the concern became known as Elton, Miles and Wilcox. However, crown glass making in Bristol was declining so rapidly that by 1810 all production seems to have ceased. It was in this year that Philip Miles, who had succeeded his father in the business, and Isaac Elton, transferred their shares to John Hilhouse Wilcox, who in turn had succeeded his father John Wilcox, and the following year he leased the bottle house to Henry Ricketts and Co, who already ran the Phoenix flint glasshouse at Templegate. An interesting commentary on the state of the buildings, which by now were a hundred years old, came from the assessor's report when the lease of the bottle house came up for renewal in 1824: '. . . on account of the very dilapidated state of the whole of the Premises would advise their being let at £250 per Annum . . .'. The comment on the adjoining glasshouse read, '. . . in their present state think them worth £60 per Annum . . .'. Whilst the crown glasshouse was to work no more, the bottle glasshouse continued as Henry Ricketts and Co until 1851, when it was taken over by Henry's son Richard and run under his name for two years, at which point an amalgamation with the adjoining glasshouse, the Hoopers, took place.

12. Avon Street (Hoopers)

This bottle glasshouse was built in 1720 by a consortium consisting of a barber-surgeon, a glassmaker, a glasshouse pot-maker, an innkeeper, a maltster, two mariners, a soap boiler, a sugar baker, three merchants and five hoopers, from whom presumably the glasshouse took its name. This partnership was large, since it was customary to limit the group to four or five, for example, a financier seeking investment, a glassmaker to control the output, a user of bottles such a brewer, distiller or wine bottler, and a merchant with a market to satisfy. The promoter of the enterprise was Robert Hiscox, the barber-surgeon, who appears to have done well at the outset since he rented one acre of land at an annual rent of nine pounds, and then leased two-thirds of this to the consortium at twelve pounds a year. The interest of the hoopers had been stimulated no doubt by the increasing trade with Portugal, following the Methuen treaty which resulted in increased exportation of empty bottles and their re-importation filled with wine.

As with other Bristol glasshouses, the Hoopers exported their products to markets other than Portugal, to southern France, the Canaries, the West Indies and to America. With so large a partnership it is not surprising that shares frequently came up for sale. In 1749, for example, the following notice appeared, '. . . four shares of the Coopers (sic) glasshouse . . . it being the sixth part of the whole . . .', and again in 1752 two shares came up for sale. Thirteen years later the following notice appeared in the *Bristol Journal:*

'For sale by auction The Hoopers Glasshouse, situate in the parish of St Philip's; with all the Buildings Outhouses and Materials, together with large quantities of Sand, Kelp, Clay, Glass. . . . This glasshouse is known to be well situated and commodious for this manufactory, has lately had a very thorough repair and lies convenient to the River with a very good wharf. The present lease has 55 years to come and is subject to a ground rent of £12 per annum.'

This was the opportunity for Richard Reynolds, his brother-in-law William Cowles, Cornelius Fry and Richard Cannington, a partnership, with the exception of Cowles, already interested in the flint glasshouse in Temple Street, to expand their interests. In 1775 Richard Cannington withdrew from the bottle making side of the partnership, whilst John Dowell, Richard Frampton and Robert Lawson joined. The glasshouse ran under various names, for example, Cowles, Dowell, Lawson and Co; Lawson, Fry, Frampton and Co; Fry, Frampton and Co, until 1809, when it was taken over by Joseph and Septimus Cookson, whose family had strong glassmaking connections at Newcastle upon Tyne.

In 1824, the year that William and Thomas Powell transferred their glass cutting and salt glaze stoneware business from Bath Parade to the Red Lane glasshouse, they joined the brothers Cookson and the Hoopers glasshouse became Cookson and Powells. Four years later Septimus Cookson died and Joseph retired in 1831, leaving the partnership in the hands of the Powell brothers, who were later joined by one of their employees, Edward Filer. At this time the adjoining Soap Boilers bottle house was in the hands of Henry Ricketts, but in 1851 his son Richard took it over and two years later amalgamated with the Hoopers glasshouse. The concern ran as Powell, Ricketts and Filer until 1856 when it became Powell and Ricketts, William Powell and Edward Filer having by then died. A. C. Powell, who later inherited the glasshouse, commented as follows:

'For a long period there had been fierce competition between the two firms, and much unfriendliness, to their mutual disadvantage. At last it was decided to unite their forces, and the event was celebrated by a feast, the relation of whose mighty proportions was a favourite subject of some of the old men.'

By the mid-century these glasshouses were the remaining evidence of glassmaking in Bristol, and they were to continue under the name Powell and Ricketts until the early 1920s, thus establishing a continuous run of over two hundred years. In the 1860s it was the first bottle glasshouse to install the Siemens furnace, a recently introduced and revolutionary system for melting glass but, as A. C. Powell comments:

> 'The problem of producing glass on the larger scale required for
> making bottles was not then solved, however, and Powell and Ricketts
> had to pass through a long and costly experience of experiments before
> success was attained.'

The period immediately following the first world war brought two
problems to glass bottle manufacturers; the depression and the need to
decide whether to introduce the automatic machinery that was then
becoming available, and so achieve greater productivity. Regrettably,
Powell and Ricketts failed to find a solution and the company went into
liquidation on July 13th, 1923.

13. Limekiln Lane

On February 2nd, 1745, the *Bristol Oracle* carried a notice that the Limekiln glasshouse was '. . . to be lett and entered upon immediately . . .'.
Situated on the bank of the Avon close to Jacob's Well and Hotwell,
this glasshouse was in an excellent position to supply the bottles that
were referred to in an advertisement in the *Freeholders Journal* in 1722.

> 'Bristol Water for sale in Bottles. The empty bottles at 2s per dozen.
> N.B. The bottles are large and London shaped.'

Buckley is of the view that it must have been in work by then since in that
year a glassmaker, William Wood, voted in the parish in which the
glasshouse stands.

The Child family were associated with the glasshouse for most of the
second half of the eighteenth century. During that time William Child,
and subsequently Richard Child, took apprentices, and Sketchley's
directory of 1775 lists a William Child as living at 38 Limekiln Lane, and
other glassmakers in the area. There are also references to a Mr Hill
through a curious statement in the *Bristol Chronicle* on April 25th, 1761.

> 'Whereas a Report generally prevails that Mr Hill at Lime Kiln
> Glasshouse had received from my shop . . . a Composition, instead of
> Glauber's Salts . . . which as soon as taken, brought on such a violent
> vomiting, etc as might have proved fatal, had not its Effects been
> prevented by taking large Quantities of Oil . . .'.

The goods had been bought elsewhere and fortunately the dose on this
occasion had not proved fatal, although some eighteen months later the
Bath Chronicle reported that 'Mr George Hill, one of the proprietors of the
Lime Kiln Glasshouse', had died. It must be hoped that there was no

connection between the two events. Life was not short of incident in this area since in June, 1764, a Mr Joshua Williams was attacked and robbed; '. . . The men at the glasshouse went to apprehend the robber . . .'. Some years later someone stole a quantity of their working tools, including seven irons on which the bottles were blown; '. . . Whoever will discover the offender shall receive a Guinea reward . . .'.

Among the pupils at Bristol Grammar School from 1771 to 1778 was John Nicholas whose address is given as the Glass House, Limekiln Lane, and the directories of 1785 and 1787 show the ownership as Child, Nicholas and Co. William Child had died in 1781 and two further members of the family, both connected with the glassworks, in 1790 and 1791. The close family interest in the glasshouse may already have waned since in the late 1780s the concern is referred to as John Nicholas and Co, and he had as partners John Robert Lucas, who had a beer and cider business in Nicholas Street, and Richard Stratton, a hooper from Denmark Street. As a bottler, Lucas would have been interested in the Limekiln glasshouse but, in addition, in 1781 he married the daughter of John Adams the manager of a glass bottle works at Stanton Wick. In 1787 Lucas took over the glasshouse. The following year he announced that he wished to dispose of his Nicholas Street business, '. . . intending to confine himself solely to the Crown Glass and Glass Bottle Manufactures . . .' which, in effect, recognised also his interest, together with Henry Pater and William Coathupe, in the first glasshouse to be built at Nailsea.

By 1793 Lucas had severed his connection with the Limekiln Lane glasshouse, and the business was carried on by John Nicholas and Richard Stratton. Two years later Stratton withdrew and John Nicholas continued alone, renewing his lease for a further forty years in 1819. The glasshouse is referred to in the report of the Commissioners of Inquiry into the Excise Tax on Glass, from which it can be seen that in 1832 they melted 380 tons of glass, which was a reasonably substantial amount for a glasshouse of that size. John Nicholas did not submit evidence to the Commissioners, but by this time he was in his 70s and living at Bath. The glasshouse did not continue working for much longer. By 1838, the site was in the hands of Thomas and Isaac Rouch, timber merchants, and the owners of the site, the Cathedral authorities, had given permission for the cone to come down.

14. Crews Hole
To the east of the city at Crews Hole a bottle glasshouse was built which,

whatever its origins, became connected with the Cheese Lane glassmaking interests of Thomas Tyndall, as is shown by an advertisement in 1766 which offered for sale by auction the equipment and stock of raw materials and a one-third share in the Crews Hole glasshouse, as well as the two Soap Boilers glasshouses. Although Tyndall continued to hold the leases all three glasshouses were in the hands of William King and Co, and the reason for the sale was the break up of the partnership between William King and Thomas Harris. Although severing his connection with the Soap Boilers glasshouses William King continued with Crews Hole until he died in 1777. As *Felix Farley's Bristol Journal* put it, '. . . he was much respected as a tradesman, and greatly lamented by the poor, to whom he was a liberal bene-factor . . .'. A Mr George Bowser continued to work the glasshouse for the executors until 1778, when it came up for auction:

> '. . . These works are deemed the most complete and conveniently situated of any in or about this City, being on the centre of the Avon and near the Coal Works (a great advantage to a Glass house factory) and a good set of hands ready for employment so that the house may be immediately set to work. . . .'

By 1795 it was again on offer '. . . by reason of the proprietors death . . .'. The bottle hands at Crews Hole must have had a torrid time during the final quarter of the eighteenth century since it was again on offer in 1797 and 1800. They were certainly considered part of the goods and chattels as the advertisement shows; '. . . in excellent repair and full working with a set of good hands and a large stock of prime pots . . .'. Prospective purchasers were referred to the '. . . Counting House in Pennywell Lane of the late Mr James Jones . . .', a well known merchant, shipowner, and in the year prior to his death, Warden of the Society of Merchant Venturers. It would seem therefore that James Jones had taken over proprietorship from William King, and combined this with an interest in both the Temple Backs bottle and the Temple Street flint glasshouses. If the directories are to be believed both the Crews Hole and the Temple Backs glasshouses ran as James Jones and Co until 1795, then as Jones and Co, and finally in 1803 the Crews Hole glasshouse is referred to as Thomas Jones and Co, after which both glasshouses appear to have ceased production.

15. Prewitt Street
The twenty feet of glasshouse cone that now forms the restaurant of the

Dragonara Hotel is the sole surviving evidence of the buildings that comprised the once thriving Bristol glass industry. Very little is known about this glasshouse, by whom it was built, and what products were made in it. The directories give no lead and the only clear evidence is that in 1780 it appears on Benning's map of Bristol, and again, that in 1812 the site was taken over by H. & T. Proctor for the manufacture of chemicals and artificial fertilizers.

16. Portwall Lane (Phoenix)

The Phoenix glasshouse in Portwall Lane was the last to be built in Bristol. The moving spirit behind its construction was the thirty-five year old Jacob Wilcox Ricketts, already in business as a tobacconist, and with Philip George, founder of the Bristol Porter Brewery. Ricketts gathered together an important group of citizens, of whom David Evans, later to be Sheriff and then Mayor of Bristol, was probably the most influential. The other partners were his brother Richard, John Wadham, a glass merchant; Richard Symes, and Thomas Morgan. It was probably the first occasion in which a consortium had no glassmaker among its partners. The glasshouse was built on the site of the Phoenix Inn, purchased in 1788 from Elizabeth, widow of Samuel Taylor who, with his brothers, had worked the Red Lane glasshouse. The following year the Phoenix glasshouse under the title Wadham, Ricketts and Co was in business, offering ' . . . a complete assortment of every article of flint-glass, which will be sold on the most reasonable terms . . .'.

In the 1780s the flint glass trade had been depressed, but there were signs of revival toward the end of the decade; this may have encouraged the Ricketts consortium to go ahead. Although there were already three flint glasshouses in Bristol, the one at Bedminster was on the point of closing down. This would have provided a source of skilled labour that otherwise might have proved difficult to obtain. The Venus glasshouse in Temple Street had recently changed ownership and by 1791 it had amalgamated with the Phoenix, with two of the three partners, James Jones, already interested in the Temple Backs and the Crews Hole glasshouses, and William Fry, a distiller and wine merchant, joining the partnership. The 1790s were a period of intense financial speculation and a number of Bristol merchants seem to have been caught up in this. By 1796 Richard Symes, Thomas Morgan and John Wadham had withdrawn, William Fry had been declared bankrupt, whilst James Jones had died. The partnership was down to Jacob Wilcox Ricketts, his brother Richard and David Evans.

Plate 28.

Scent Bottle, W. & T. Powell, Red Lane Glasshouse, c1825–30.
Flint glass, wheel-cut. G 625. Ht. 14.5 cm. Given by A. C. Powell (see note on plate 25): making and
cutting similarly attributed to Bristol. Like all this group of pieces, the quality of the metal is remarkably
brilliant and rich, a necessity for such deep cutting. Two glass crowns are illustrated in Greethead's *1831
Coronation Procession* (see plate 13), which shows the glassmakers in procession: this perhaps indicates a
link with the design.
See page 37.

Billhead of Powell Bros. & Co., Hoopers Glasshouse, c1830–50. Signed by the engraver 'Drake Sc.(ulpit) Bristol'. TA 5001.
Outside the glasshouse are shown the processes of bottle-making at the furnace: 'gathering' hot glass at the furnace; rolling or 'marvering' the bubble; blowing it into the mould in the ground (opened by a foot pedal); shaping the neck; stacking the completed bottle to cool gradually.
See page 52.

Plate 29.

Plate 30.

Billhead of Henry Ricketts & Co., c1821–51.
Signed by the engraver 'T. Radclyffe Sc.(ulpit)/Birmingham'. TA 4628.
Bristol's ship and castle supports the phoenix, symbolising the Phoenix Glasshouse in Portwall Lane, illustrated to the right: to the left are a glasshouse and merchant ship symbolising trade. The two bottle types illustrate Henry Ricketts' new method of moulding, patented in 1821, which profoundly affected the industry. See also plate 40 for a similar wine bottle (N 1785), and plate 41 for a similar porter bottle (G 3225).
See page 56.

The remaining competitor, the flint glasshouse on Redcliff Backs, had been taken over by George Daubeny and John Cave, and in 1802 it was merged with the Phoenix glasshouse. John Cave's son with the same name had replaced his father, who had died, and he together with George Daubeny joined the partnership, as did Jacob Wilcox Ricketts' son Henry, who replaced his uncle Richard. Nine years later the partnership took over the Soap Boilers bottle glasshouse in Cheese Lane.

After a slow start the glasshouse became very profitable. When David Evans died in 1816 his share capital had almost quadrupled over a period of some fourteen years. The financial year 1818/19 was the most successful the company was to have, with a profit of £7,200. Two years later a loss of £7,122 was recorded, and the halcyon days were over. This was the year in which both the flint glass and the bottle trade slumped severely, and it was the year in which the relationship between Henry Ricketts and his father, which had been deteriorating for some years, took a bitter turn.

In 1825 Jacob Wilcox Ricketts resigned from the company he had created, and the partnership was reformed with Henry Glascodine, secretary and accountant, and John Gunning, glasshouse manager, joining Henry Ricketts and John Cave. Jacob Wilcox Ricketts' share of the concern was valued at £22,291. His investment had given him, at least, a net profit of twenty per cent a year over the previous twenty-one years. In a sense the resignation of Jacob Wilcox Ricketts marked the end of the great days of the Phoenix glasshouse, although it was to continue for a further 26 years.

John Cave died in 1842 and was succeeded by his son William, and John Gunning retired the following year through ill health. In 1845 Henry Ricketts' son Richard joined the partnership and he and Henry Glascodine were designated to manage the glasshouses. But since the departure of Jacob Wilcox Ricketts the fortunes of the company had been mixed. From 1841 to 1845 losses were very heavy, and although the next three years were profitable, further losses were incurred from 1849 to 1851, with the result that the glasshouse closed.

The demise of the Phoenix glasshouse spelt the end of flint glassmaking in Bristol, and of the sixteen glasshouses that had been built only two bottle houses remained, and they were soon to amalgamate. Henry Ricketts could find no buyer, and he was to write in May, 1854:

'The premises have been advertised several times – the Rent required
as feiffed by the late Mr Cave has been £500 – there has been no offer for

them. This rent (although reduced from that paid by H.R. & Co) has
no doubt been a barrier – the Flint and Bottle Glass Trades have been
in a very flourishing state since the concern was closed.'

It was, in a sense, a sad ending to a glasshouse that had contributed
much to the reputation of Bristol in the world of glassmaking. The
quarrel between Henry Ricketts and his father undoubtedly had an effect
upon its fortunes, but the prime cause of the demise of the Phoenix
glasshouse, as with all the Bristol glasshouses, was that the industry was
moving inexorably to the developing industrial areas of the midlands
and the north. Yet the Phoenix glasshouse had made its contribution to
technical development with John Donaldson in 1802, for example,
following the Perrotts with a patent for a more efficient furnace, and
Henry Ricketts, in 1821, with a bottle mould patent by which the shape
of a bottle could be controlled more precisely than by way of the methods
then in use, a design that has ever since born his name.

Bibliography

Abbreviations:

BGAS Bristol and Gloucestershire Archaeological Society

BRL Bristol Reference Library **BRO** Bristol Record Office

BRS Bristol Record Society **GT** Glass Technology

JSGT Journal of the Society of Glass Technology

For detailed studies of the glass industry in Bristol see:

Alford, B. W. E. *The flint and bottle glass industry in the early 19th century: a case study of a Bristol firm*
Business History, v 10, 1968, pp 12–21

Buckley, F. *The early glasshouses of Bristol*
JSGT, v 9, 1925, pp 36–61

Charleston, R. J. *Michael Edkins and the problem of English enamelled glass*
JSGT, v 38, 1954, pp 3T-16T

Hughes, G. B. *English, Scottish and Irish table glass*
London, 1956. In particular chapter 21, Bristol-blue glass

Hughes, G. B. *The heyday of Bristol enamel glass*
Country Life, 1961, p 512

Jones, O. *The contribution of the Ricketts' mould to the manufacture of the English wine bottle, 1820–1850*
Journal of Glass Studies, v 25, 1983, pp 167–177

Josephs, Z. *The Jacobs of Bristol, glassmakers to King George III*
BGAS, v 95, 1978, pp 98–101

Powell, A. C. *Glassmaking in Bristol*
BGAS, v 47, 1926, pp 211–257

Scott, A. & C. *Blue glass from Bristol*
Country Life, 1961, p 327

Whitting, J. C. *Notes on Lowdin's glasshouse, Redcliff Hill*
BRL B26224, 1969

Webb, F. G. *Bristol glassmakers.* Notes on Bristol History No. 8
University of Bristol: Dept. of Extra-Mural Studies, 1968

Weeden, C. *The Bristol bottlemakers*
Chemistry and Industry, 1978, pp 378–381
The problems of consolidation in the Bristol flint glass industry
GT, v 22, 1981, pp 236–238

The Ricketts family and the Phoenix glasshouse, Bristol
The Glass Circle, v 4, 1982, pp 84–101
The Bristol glass industry: its rise and decline
GT, v 24, 1983, pp 241–258

The Bristol Record Office holds various documents on the glass industry, for example:

Phoenix glasshouse	MS 12143
Redcliff Backs and St Thomas Street glasshouses	MS 12143 (41)
Hoopers glasshouse wages sheets	MS 35469 (1)
A. C. Powell – private notes	MS 35469 (2)
Temple Street flint glasshouse	MS 00401 (6)

Information on the glasshouses and their owners can be obtained from contemporary Bristol newspapers, Directories such as Arrowsmith, Browne, Mathews, Routh, Shiercliff and Sketchley, copies of which are held at the Bristol Reference Library.

The sites of the glasshouses can be seen from various maps of the city, particularly those published by Ashmead, Donne, Mathews, Millerd and Rocque. The Bristol City Museum and the Bristol Reference Library hold copies.

A number of publications on the glass industry contain either references to Bristol, or to events that affected the glass industry in Bristol, for example:

Brown, C. M.	*The glass industry in the 1830s* GT, v 21, 1980, pp 184–189
Court, W. H. B.	*The rise of the Midland industries 1600–1838* London, 1938
Davies, P.	*The development of the American glass industry* Cambridge, Mass., 1949
Guttery, D. R.	*From broad glass to cut crystal* London, 1956
Hartshorne, A.	*Old English glasses* London, 1897
Meigh, E.	*The story of the glass bottle* Stoke on Trent, 1972
Scoville, W. C.	*Revolution in glassmaking* Cambridge, Mass., 1948
Thorpe, W. A.	*English glass* London, 1961
HMSO	*13th Report of the Commissioners of Inquiry into the Excise Establishment – Glass* London, 1835

Below is a list of those publications which either contain references to the glass industry in Bristol or, in dealing with economic, commercial or political matters in the 18th and 19th centuries, outline the scenario in which the glass industry in Bristol developed and then declined:

Buchanan, A. &   *Industrial archaeology of the Bristol region*
Cossons, N.   Newton Abbot, 1969

Defoe, D.   *A tour through the whole island of Great Britain*
                   London, 1971, ed. Rogers, P.

Latimer, J.   *Annals of Bristol in the 18th century*
                   Bristol, 1893

Little, B.   *The city and county of Bristol*
                   London, 1954

McGrath, P. (ed.) *Merchants and merchandise in 17th century Bristol*
                   BRS, v 19, 1955

MacInnes, C. M.   *Bristol: a gateway of Empire*
                   Newton Abbot, 1968

Marcy, P. T.   *Bristol's roads and communications on the eve of the industrial revolution 1740–80.* BGAS, v 87, 1968, pp 149–172

Minchinton, W. E. *The trade of Bristol in the 18th century*
                   BRO, v 20, 1957

Williams, A. F.   *Bristol port plans and improvement schemes of the 18th century*
                   BGAS, v 81, 1962, pp 138–181

Alford, B. W. E.   *The economic development of Bristol in the 19th century: an enigma.* Contained in Essays in Bristol and Gloucestershire History, ed. McGrath, P. & Cannon, J. BGAS, 1976

There are occasional references to glassmaking in some early histories of Bristol, for example:

Barrett, W.   *History and antiquities of Bristol*, Bristol, 1789
Nicholls, J. F. & *Bristol past and present*, Bristol, 1881
Taylor, J.
Taylor, J.   *Book about Bristol*, Bristol, 1872

Beer bottle, Powell & Ricketts, Avon Street Glasshouse, late 19th/early 20th century. Body moulded 'POWELL & RICKETTS/ BOTTLE/ MANUFACTURERS BRISTOL' about a phoenix, within an oval encircled by 'REGISTERED/TRADE MARK'. N 9330. Ht. 24.7 cm.
From 1853 the partnership became Powell and Ricketts, which continued until 1923, when the firm dissolved.
See page 51.

Token of Powell, Ricketts and Filer, Soapboilers Glasshouse, Cheese Lane, c1853–6. G 2154.
Between 1811 and about 1815, difficulties at the Mint meant that employers were permitted to issue tokens in lieu of coins in short supply, a practice which continued. The partnership of Powell, Ricketts and Filer ended the rivalry between Ricketts & Co. at the Soapboilers Glasshouse and their neighbours at the Hoopers Glasshouse, Powell and Filer.
See page 52.

Plate 31.

Plate 32.

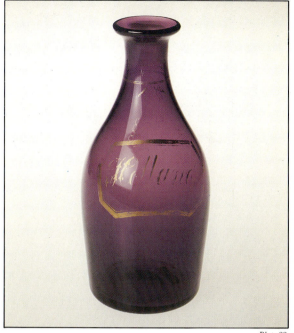

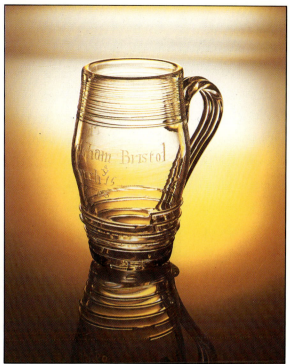

Plate 33.

Plate 34.

'Hollands' Decanter, Wadham Ricketts & Co., Phoenix Glasshouse, 1789.
Amethyst glass, enriched with gilding: base acid-etched 'Wadham Ricketts & Co. 1789'. Stopper missing. N 8777. Ht. 17.7 cm.
The only example at present known of amethyst glass documented to Bristol: Isaac Jacobs however advertised in *Felix Farley's Bristol Journal* a dessert set "in burnished Gold upon Royal Purple colored Glass". The partnership was founded in this year.
See page 56.

The 'Goldham' Mug, probably Bristol, 1760.
Flint glass, with trailed decoration at rim and foot: the barrel-shaped body wheel-engraved 'Martha Goldham Bristol/Novem ye 15/1760'. N 8000. Ht. 10.5 cm.
Perhaps a christening mug: the spontaneous trailed decoration suggests a relatively unsophisticated customer for this simple piece.

Plate 35.

Two jugs, W. & T. Powell, Red Lane Glasshouse, c1825.
Flint glass, wheel-cut. G 605, G 606. Ht. 16.7 cm., 13.4 cm.
Given by A. C. Powell: according to inventory, made by Badger's of Dudley and cut in Bristol (see A. C. Powell, *Glassmaking in Bristol,* p 227). A similar jug to G 606 appears in Greethead's *1831 Coronation Procession* (see plate 13), with hob-nail cut body and deeply curved rim.

Plate 36.

'Phoenix' Goblet, Ricketts, Evans & Co., Phoenix Glasshouse, c1814.
Flint glass, wheel-engraved 'PEACE & PLENTY' within olive sprays,
on reverse, 'PHOENIX GLASSHOUSE'. N 5055. Ht. 19.9 cm.
Traditionally this goblet commemorates the Peace of Paris of 1814,
during the Napoleonic Wars. The goblet's proportion is typical of the
larger bowl and shorter, knopped stem of the early 19th century.
See page 56.

Plate 37.

Billhead of Vigor & Stevens, Redcliff Backs. 1786.
Unsigned. Mb 3765. Made out to Mr. C. W. Viner and dated 'September 20 1786'.
Earlier advertisements imply the production of high quality flint glass here, including coloured ware. Robert Vigor's connection with the firm dates from 1767, but his name continued to be used after his death in 1782 until about 1789. By 1770 he had been joined by Stevens, and in 1793 a dispute seems to have caused the departure of James Stevens, leaving William Stevens still a partner until 1798.
See page 36.

Billhead of Stevens, Randolph & Co., Redcliff Backs. c1793.
Signed by the engraver 'Doddrell Sculpt.'. MB 3766.
By the same engraver as the contemporary billhead of Wadham Ricketts & Co. (see plate 17, Mb 3763), for the Phoenix Glasshouse. This partnership was brief under this name, though Randolph had been involved since 1789, lasting less than a year. With the arrival of John Cave and George Daubeny, it became Stevens, Cave & Co. In 1802 the firm amalgamated with Wadham Ricketts & Co. then of Portwall Lane, closing thereafter.
See page 36.

Plate 38.

A VIEW of St. VINCENTS ROCKS with the HOT WELL's from Mr Warrens House the Opposite South side of the River Avon

A : St Vincents Rocks   B : the Hot Wells   C : Mr Warrens House

Plate 39.

A View of St. Vincents Rocks with the Hot Well's from Mr. Warren's House, from Rocque's Map of Bristol. c1742 (see plate 8, M 768). City of Bristol Museum and Art Gallery.

This vignette appears as part of the border of the map, showing an early 18th century view of the Redcliff Gate glasshouse, run by Richard Warren in conjunction with the St. Thomas Street glasshouse. It was demolished in 1718 *(see page 37),* and may have been a bottle house.

AMERICA and the BRISTOL GLASS TRADE

THE GLASSHOUSES of Bristol enjoyed a considerable trade with America in the eighteenth century, providing much of the window glass, bottles, and table glass needed by the colonists. The Bristol Port Books offer some evidence of the extent of this trade: for just the month of June, 1741, there were recorded over 10,000 bottles and 27 chests of window glass bound for American ports. The prosperity that Bristol's merchants and manufacturers derived from the American market was threatened in the 1760s and 1770s by the passage of the Stamp Act and the Townshend Acts. The latter measure levied duties on glass, among other articles. Petitioning Parliament early in 1775, Bristol's Society of Merchant Venturers noted that although the repeal of those acts somewhat revived business, 'other measures lately adopted, caused such a great uneasiness in the minds of the inhabitants of America as to make the merchants apprehensive of the most alarming consequences and which, if not speedily remedied, must involve them in utter ruin.'[1] As they feared, the colonists revolted and the war curtailed the overseas trade. As will be seen, however, at least one Bristol glasshouse was able to capitalize on the Loyalist market.

By the 1790s the exportation of glasswares to America had resumed. The Bristol manufacturers discovered, however, they now had to compete with inexpensive Continental glass as well as the products of America's own glasshouses.[2] Although glass had been made in America from 1608, it was only after the second war with Great Britain, 1812–14, that the industry became securely established. Ironically, Bristol had a role to play in this development. Glassblowers trained there were among those who travelled across the Atlantic, bringing the traditions and technology of the Bristol factories.

The picture of Bristol's glass trade with America is a fragmentary one, because only a handful of documents survive to suggest the nature and extent of America's reliance on the Bristol glasshouses. Importing merchants received quantities of English glassware, not only from Bristol, but also from London, Liverpool, and Newcastle-on-Tyne. In their newspaper advertisements they rarely specified which glassmaking centre was their source. Very often, the glass they sold was merely described as 'English'. The papers of several glass merchants have fortunately been preserved and contain detailed information about their Bristol connections. These, and a variety of other primary sources, provide the basis for the following discussion.

Window glass was imported from Bristol by a number of American merchants, for general stock as well as for particular customers' needs. An early reference to Bristol window glass in the colonies occurs in the invoice book of Philadelphian Samuel Powel, who in 1724/5 travelled to England and purchased there, for his father, two boxes of 8 by 10-inch panes of Bristol glass. Philadelphia newspapers of the 1730s carry several advertisements that mention Bristol window glass, including those of George McCall, Teague and Hillier, and Willing and Shippen. These were not glass merchants *per se* but general importers who sold a broad range of goods. Thomas Sharp, for example, notified the public in 1734 that he had recently imported from Bristol 'all sorts of Window Glass' as well as raisins, prunes, and indentured servants. Merchants who sold drugs and apothecary ware often had window glass to sell, as in the case of Gerardus Duykinck at the sign of the Looking-Glass and Druggist Pot in New York, who advertised London and Bristol crown glass in 1766.[3]

It is somewhat ironic that Philadelphia's only glass manufacturer in the 1750s, Richard Wistar (1727–81), was also an importer of Bristol window glass. The indifference of his Bristol correspondents, however, insured the imports would remain but a minor part of his business. Wistar was the Quaker proprietor of Wistarburgh, America's first successful glassworks. Founded in 1738 by his father, a German immigrant named Caspar Wistar (1696–1752), the glasshouse was situated in Salem County, New Jersey, some forty-five miles down the Delaware River from Philadelphia. Four glassblowers came over from Germany as partners in the undertaking to build and operate the factory. The Wistars continued to rely on German-trained craftsmen during the forty years Wistarburgh remained in operation.[4] This was the situation throughout America in the colonial period: the glass industry was dominated by German artisans who struggled to compete in a market accustomed to the quality and styles of English imports. Like most colonial factories, Wistarburgh concentrated on the manufacture of bottles and window glass made by the cylinder method. Some hollow ware was commercially produced; several sugar bowls, candlesticks, and other forms of green, blue, and colourless glass have been attributed to the Wistar enterprise.

It is not known whether Caspar Wistar was actively importing English glass to sell in his Philadelphia store along with his own products. Recorded in his receipt book in 1753, the year after his death, is his widow's purchase of £32 2s. 6d. worth of 'Winder Glass' from ship captain James Child. It was because of Child that Richard Wistar first wrote to Samuel Taylor and Brothers of Bristol, early in 1759.[5] Child had assured Wistar that the Taylors at their glasshouse Without Templegate would serve him well and 'on as Low terms as any person in Bristol can doo.' At the same time, Wistar wrote to his agents in Bristol, American merchant William Freeman and his Birmingham partner, John Oseland, asking the lowest prices of Bristol crown glass as he expected he would need a large quantity every year.

Wistar saw an advantage, however, in dealing directly with the manufacturer. He was familiar with the Taylors' products, having bought from Child several parcels of window glass that had been consigned to him by Daniel Taylor, Senior. 'In Many boxes,' Wistar observed, 'there are many [squares] Lacking a Corner which is a Great Disadvantage to Sale.' He wanted the glass to be 'Strait & Well Packed which has Not been the Case with Great Quantities Lately Sent from Your Place Many boxes haveing from 20 to 60 Panes brocken.' At this time he ordered, and enclosed partial remittance for, thirty boxes of window glass panes of 8 by 10-inch size and five boxes of 7 by 9, each box to contain one hundred feet. Whether the Taylors were annoyed by Wistar's demands and complaints or were having operational difficulties is not clear, but no glass was shipped. The firm did send an invoice in March, 1759, which arrived in Philadelphia the following November, but no window glass accompanied the invoice. Wistar was disappointed and wrote, 'I have been out of Window Glass for 2 mo[nths] past & Severall of my own Workman have been Sick so that the Disappointment has effect[ed] me the More.' Nonetheless, Wistar expanded his initial order by requesting fifty-two more boxes of glass and fifty squares of large-size panes. Wistar reiterated his concern that the panes be 'as Strait & Clear as Possible . . . as they are for fraims.' Still the Taylors were silent: they sent no glass nor did they send any letter to explain the delay. On May 12th, 1760, Wistar expressed his irritation, saying '[it]Appears as if you had no Inclination of supplying me with any Glass if this be the Case [I] Should have been Glad had I been Informed thereof as I imagine that I might have Supply'd from some other House Ere this.' He pointed out to the Taylors the foolishness of their neglect, noting that they would have had several more orders from him by now had they served him promptly. To encourage them to act, Wistar offered to send cash with his future orders – but only if the first shipment ever came to hand. Obviously frustrated by their treatment of him, Wistar complained

'I desire You to Inform me Whether I may Rely on You[r] House for Glass or not, as I find my Demand and Trade to Encrease Shall want about 3 hundred boxes Yearly. if Such a Correspondent be worth your Notice other wise I must be obliged to Try some other houses I am Out at Present (& have been So for 6m[onths] past) of all sort of Bristol Glass.

That same day he wrote to Freeman and Oseland, hoping they could arrange for some window glass to be sent to him. In spite of his difficulties with the Taylors, Wistar believed theirs was the best window glass in Bristol, with that of Thomas Warren the second best. Freeman and Oseland attended to Wistar's request immediately and shipped on board the *Ann George* some 1,500 feet of window glass. The 8 by 10-inch size cost Wistar 3½d. per foot, while the 7 by 9 was 3¼d., and the 6 by 8, 2¾d. From Samuel and Daniel Taylor Wistar heard nothing, so that in July, 1761, he demanded that they surrender to his agents the money he had paid, with interest. Wistar added, 'I am Sorry You have Given me the Occasion to Say thay you have not behaved Like Gentl[men] Nor Yett like men of Veracity.'

Other Philadelphia merchants seem to have had more successful relationships with the glass manufacturers of Bristol. Christopher Marshall and Son, for example, were druggists who also sold paints and window glass. Bristol crown and common glass appears in their advertisements as early as 1748. When the firm became Christopher and Charles Marshall in 1765, an inventory of their stock was taken. Eighty-seven per cent of their window glass was Bristol-made, with the remainder from London and Newcastle. After 1765 Bristol became the sole source of the Marshalls' window glass. They received large shipments from Samuel Taylor and Son, Warren and Company, and Warrens, Cannington, Reynolds, and Cowles. From the Bristol house of Longman and Vigor the Philadelphia druggists purchased vials and glass urinals.[6]

That last-named factory commenced the production of crown glass in the 1770s under the name of Vigor and Stevens. Between 1775 and 1782, when it was known as Vigor, Stevens, and Hill, this establishment notified its customers in America – as well as on the Continent – that they would henceforth brand their packages with 'VSH'. This was so their crown glass could be readily distinguished from that of the other two manufactories in Bristol. An invoice survives from September, 1789, when the factory was owned by Vigor, Stevens, Randolph, and Stevens.[7] This documents the shipment on board the *Lively* of forty boxes of window glass of various sizes to Stewart and Jones, American merchants. Both the 8 by 10 and 9 by 11 panes were priced at 5d. per foot, and the 6 by 8 ones were 3½d. Boxes for shipping cost £3 3s. 6d., while insurance, bills of lading, and other charges added another £2 3s. 2d.

In the nineteenth century, even as America's own crown glass factories grew, Bristol window glass continued to be in demand. One New York importer advertised a shipment of 2,000 boxes of Bristol glass of all sizes in 1810. That same year a man building a house in Hanover, New Hampshire, was trying to decide between the Boston and the Bristol crown – largely on the basis of price.[8] A number of merchants carried Bristol as well as domestic window glass. B. C. Attwood of Portland, Maine, for example, advertised in 1819 that he had window glass from Keene, New Hampshire, as well as the Bristol crown. That Bristol's product was the most popular of the English window glass is implied by the 1825 New York market listing which includes Bristol as the only foreign window glass.[9]

Bristol flat glass was also exported to America for uses other than windows. In a letter of 1752, Hugh Roberts, representing the Wardens of the Pennsylvania Hospital in Philadelphia, asked Charles Willing to acquire from Bristol five hundred feet of 'good' glass for the Hospital's lamps. The glass was to be strong and 'as free from winding as possible for its to be put in Tin Channels or Grooves that are already made.' Roberts specified two sizes of trapezoidal panes in which the glass was to be cut, but did not name a particular factory.[10]

Bottles formed a very important part of Bristol's export trade with America. 'Pipes, glass and bottles' from Bristol were sold by Messrs. Banister at their Boston store in 1712. Merchants throughout America continued to advertise Bristol bottles in the eighteenth century and well into the nineteenth. Benjamin W. Rodgers and Company of New York, for example, had an extensive business, with no less than three shipments of Bristol bottles arriving between July and December, 1810. Their December 17th notice listed 500 hampers of porter and wine bottles and 30 hampers of claret bottles, with each hamper holding 144 bottles.[11]

In 1765 an estate appraiser in Philadelphia recorded '16 empty Bristol bottles.' Whether the Bristol-made bottles were truly distinctive and easily recognizable at that date is not clear: 'Bristol bottles' could have been a generic term for all English bottles. After 1821, however, it may have indicated a preference for the fully-moulded bottles produced under patent by Henry Ricketts and Company. It was probably the Ricketts' bottle to which the New York firm of Masters and Markoe referred when they advertised, 'Bristol Patent quart and pint Porter Bottles/ D[itt]o old shape pint bottles.'[12] That it was, in any case, desirable to have Bristol, as opposed to other bottles made in imitation, is indicated by the advertisements of Mayer and Lohman, who in the summer of 1825 received '75 hampers genuine Bristol Bottles' at their Philadelphia warehouse. Similarly, J. G. Stacey notified the public that he had on hand 50 hampers of 'real' Bristol porter bottles from the Lucas glassworks. In 1827, the Boston Glass Bottle Company assured their customers that their product was 'of a quality equal to Bristol Bottles.'[13]

The tremendous range of bottle types offered by the Bristol glasshouses is evidenced in the 'Invoice of Sundrys' shipped from Vigor and Stevens to the Marshalls.[14] The nine crates of merchandise included over 23,000 green glass vials from ½- to 8-ounce capacity and 'thumb' [size?] vials. Regardless of size, the vials cost 8s. per 240. White or colourless glass vials were priced at 8s. 6d. Vigor and Stevens shipped lavender water bottles and Hungary vials, for the restorative Hungary water distilled from wine and rosemary leaves. Half-pint 'Belly'd' bottles of unspecified function cost 10s. per 144. For their drug business the Marshalls needed 'Small Fine' Turlington bottles at 15s. per 144. Robert Turlington's Balsam of Life, first patented in 1744, was a popular panacea of the eighteenth and nineteenth centuries.[15] In response to the Marshalls' request for 'Bannister' vials, Vigor and Stevens sent what they called 'Bandelier' vials, 'which we suppose is what you call by the Name of Bannisters Vials.'[16] Other apothecary ware was sent including green glass salt-mouth vials, white funnels, flint mortars and pestles, nipple glasses, and piped breast glasses.

Bristol table glass was advertised in America as early as 1719, when 'drinking Glasses, Decanters imported from Bristol' were offered for sale in Boston. It was quite common for colonial merchants to import glass from several English cities so it is often unclear from their advertisements which ware emanated from Bristol. Lewis DeBlois, for example, notified the public in 1761 that he had just received from London *and* Bristol several hogsheads of the 'best' engraved and flowered wineglasses and decanters.[17] Individual glassworks are rarely if ever named in the newspapers and few merchants' records exist to document the trade and production of specific houses.

Extensive papers have been preserved for one New York glass and china merchant of the late colonial era, Frederick Rhinelander (1743–

1805).[18] From them it is evident that the flint glass factory of Vigor and Stevens at Redcliff Backs was among the leaders in the American trade at that time. Rhinelander was one of several merchants in New York who specialized in glass and ceramics in the decade before the Revolutionary War.[19] Because he remained loyal to the Crown, Rhinelander, in partnership with his brother Philip, was able to continue in business with little competition during the war years when the city was under British control. Sir William Howe had taken New York on September 15th, 1776. Three-quarters of the population had fled, leaving behind some 5,000 Loyalist citizens. The arrival of British and Hessian troops as well as Loyalist refugees from other colonies swelled the city's population to 40,000 by 1783. The British evacuated New York on November 25th, 1783, after peace was declared.

For this diverse clientele Rhinelander imported English earthenware and stoneware, China trade porcelain, looking glasses, some hardware, and glassware. Before the war Rhinelander had enjoyed a considerable market in New England, wholesaling to merchants there. During the Revolution and occupation of New York, Rhinelander conducted a primarily retail business from his store on Burling's Slip on the east side of Manhattan. His customers included the Royal Governor, William Tryon, as well as Howe and other military personnel.

In his ceramics trade, Rhinelander dealt mostly with middlemen, but for his glass he corresponded directly with the manufacturers. From the beginning he favoured the glasshouses of Bristol. Freight charges were lower from Liverpool, however, and because his orders from the Staffordshire potteries were shipped from that port, Rhinelander decided in 1776 to see if a Liverpool glassworks could supply his needs instead. He placed a modest order with Josiah Perrin at the Bank Quay factory in Warrington but warned him that he had 'seen many Invoices of Glass Ware from Liverpool, but none equal to what I have from the Makers in Bristol.' The Liverpool shipment was as unsatisfactory as Rhinelander anticipated, both with regard to quality and price. Two years later Rhinelander tried again, this time ordering a small amount through one of his Liverpool ceramics agents, William Kenyon. Whether or not the shipment met with Rhinelander's approval is not known, but it was the last of the Liverpool orders. He wrote to a Stourbridge glassmaker about acquiring glass in 1780 as a favour to a correspondent, but nothing came of it. Rhinelander was quite content with his Bristol connection and advised the Stourbridge man, 'we are now – have been for a number of years supplied by one house in Bristol, and that we shall not alter the Course of our trade unless we could be supplied on better terms.'[20]

The house to which Rhinelander referred was that of Vigor and Stevens. Between 1773 and 1782, the New York importer placed at least seven large orders with that company. In 1772 he had purchased some glass from Richard Cannington at the Temple Gate glassworks in Bristol, but after that time he was loyal to Vigor and Stevens. He even informed them of his experiment with the Liverpool manufacturers, assuring them that Liverpool's 'fine Glass is so much inferior to yours and so unsuitable to the present consumption that it will not do to have Glass from that market.'[21] Moreover, Perrin charged 2s. 6d. for a dozen dram bottles instead of the usual 8d. Rhinelander did try to secure better prices from Vigor and Stevens by claiming that his Stourbridge correspondent offered him tumblers and cut glass at prices lower than Bristol's.

Although Rhinelander's stock before and during the war was composed chiefly of table glass, he had a market for small bottles. Besides the green dram bottles, he imported green and flint vials from ½- to 8-ounce capacity. For his customers in the British military Rhinelander bought 'white or flint' square bottles of several sizes that were 'suitable for canteens.'

Rhinelander sold very little window glass. In the order to Vigor and Stevens dated September 15th, 1780, he requested over 80 boxes of window panes of all dimensions and asked for another 20 boxes when he wrote again early in 1781. None of it may have arrived in New York because in a letter of January 25th, 1782, Rhinelander alludes to the capture of the *Dimsdale* which was carrying his window glass from Vigor and Stevens. He regretted this misfortune of war, because the glass 'would have come to a very good Market.'

The strongest demand in Rhinelander's New York market was for drinking vessels and these constituted the largest portion of Vigor and Steven's exports. Of the 1,021 dozen items shipped in 1777, for example, 879 or 86% of them were tumblers, mugs, and stemmed ware.

Tumblers were described as of common, flint, and double flint quality and ranged in size from half-gill to one quart. For what was apparently a special order, Rhinelander asked that the half-pint and pint size tumblers be 'very short.' Although the term 'firing glass' does not occur in the Rhinelander Papers, some tumblers may have been of this sort because of Rhinelander's request in 1779 that the half-gill tumblers have 'very stout thick bottoms.' Some of the largest tumblers ordered that year were to have covers. Only a small proportion of the tumblers sent from Bristol were decorated. Some were merely 'cut,' or described as 'cut very neat.' In 1780 Rhinelander sold ones of a 'cut diamond pattern,' and tumblers were among the forms ordered in 1782 as part of a set, each piece of which was to be 'cut with a star and beaded neat.'

On several occasions Rhinelander ordered tumblers 'with handles,' but elsewhere he used the terms mug and can. From half-pint to quart, cans were to be of both 'Upright' and 'Silver Shape,' i.e. of cylindrical and baluster form.

Vigor and Stevens provided Rhinelander's store with several different kinds of stemmed drinking glasses. What were called 'wines' came in common, flint, and best flint qualities. Many were to be small in size. In a 1778 order Rhinelander specified wines with 'short shank, not to exceed four inches in height.' More often he described such wines as 'dwarf.' For claret Rhinelander needed glasses with even shorter stems. So that Vigor and Stevens would have no doubt as to what he wanted, Rhinelander made a sketch of the claret glass in his 1780 and 1781 orders. The drawing (see plate 43) shows a large, conical bowl set on a rudimentary stem and round foot – appearing to be what is called a rummer.[22] In other orders, however, Rhinelander did use the term rummer, but it was to denote a glass of half-pint capacity. Claret glasses came in pint as well as half-pint sizes. In 1782 Rhinelander wrote Vigor and Stevens for clarets with square feet.

From his Bristol supplier Rhinelander received glasses designed for other beverages such as ale, beer, cider, lemonade, porter, punch, and water. The lemonades were of can shape, while the punch glasses had handles. Rhinelander not only carried water goblets but also 'wine and water' glasses. That these were stemmed glasses is seen in the 1776 order where they are listed as having cut and other style 'shanks' or stems. Rhinelander bought Spanish wineglasses from Vigor and Stevens, the exact form of which is not known.

Some of the wine and other stemmed drinking glasses had enamel-twist stems, but the declining fashion for this style in the 1770s is illustrated in the Rhinelander correspondence. The invoice sent from Vigor and Stevens in 1773 enumerates common wines with 'diamond' stems, which may have been facet-cut in a diamond pattern. They were sold to Rhinelander at the same price as plain stems, viz. 4s. a dozen. Dwarf wines with 'cut' stems in the same shipment cost 5s. In 1778 Rhinelander ordered wines with 'cut shanks, beaded.' This may refer to stems cut in vertical panels heightened along the edges with vertical rows of tiny circles or ovals.

The bowl styles for wineglasses named in the Rhinelander Papers are globe, lemon, and pear. Globe bowls must have been of hemispherical shape, while 'lemon' may have referred to what is known today as ogee. Pear bowls, mentioned only in 1782, could have been of the pan-top sort. Vigor and Stevens provided some wines with bowls that were flowered, i.e. wheel-engraved with floral motifs. Such engraving added 1s. 6d. to the cost per dozen. There are a few listings of enamelled wines which may mean enamel-painted bowls rather than enamel-twist stems. In 1775 Rhinelander sold some mason's glasses, which doubtless were wineglasses engraved on the bowl with the symbols of freemasonry. Although no inscribed or commemorative glasses are specified in the records, it is possible that small wineglasses engraved with Loyalist sentiments were made in Bristol and sold in New York.[23]

Decanters were another staple of Rhinelander's market. Most were needed in half-pint, pint, and quart sizes, though on one occasion, probably as a special order, Rhinelander had decanters of half-gallon and gallon sizes sent from Bristol. The 1773 invoice of Vigor and Stevens lists decanters as either champagne or sugar loaf. While the first term could denote vessels designed particularly to hold champagne, possibly with a pocket for ice, it more likely referred to a shape. 'Sugar loaf' aptly describes a style of decanter which parallels the tapered cylindrical mould in which sugar loaves were formed. By 1781 Rhinelander was asking Vigor and Stevens for decanters of the 'new sugar loaf' style, indicating that the form had been further refined. For the remainder of the decanters ordered at that time, Rhinelander wanted ones of barrel shape. He first asked Vigor and Stevens for decanters of an 'oval or egg' shape in 1779. His sketch of an oval decanter (plate 44) shows a longer neck than the sugar loaf and a body curved in at the base.

Nearly half of the decanters shipped by the Bristol factory in 1773 lacked stoppers. Three of the thirty-seven dozen described as champagne had 'ground bottoms and cut stoppers.' While these were priced by the dozen at 3s. 6d. for the quart size, the decanters that did not have ground bottoms were charged by weight, at 8d. per pound. Ground bottoms probably meant that the pontil marks were ground and polished away.

Like the drinking vessels, decanters were available in New York in plain, engraved, and cut versions. Vigor and Stevens sent two dozen decanters 'labell'd,' i.e., engraved with the name of the liquid they were

Group of three bottles, Henry Ricketts & Co., c1821–51.
These three examples illustrate the new patent moulded bottle. Left to right: wine bottle sealed with coronet over 'C', base moulded 'H. RICKETTS & CO/ GLASSWORKS BRISTOL', shoulder moulded 'PATENT' (N 1785); wine bottle sealed 'W. Leman/Chard/1771', base and shoulder moulded as previous example (T 8263, ht. 28.3 cm.); bottle, base moulded as previous two examples (T 9959, ht. 19.1 cm.).
The bottle dated 1771 is a reminder of the difficulty of dating bottles, since its post-1821 construction contradicts its 1771 seal date.
See page 56.

Plate 40.

Group of four bottles, from the Powell and Ricketts concerns, c1821–51.
Left to right: porter bottle, base moulded 'P & R BRISTOL' (G 3583, ht. 25 cm.); porter bottle, base moulded 'POWELL & CO BRISTOL (NX 809, ht. 24 cm.); wine bottle, base moulded 'H. RICKETTS BRISTOL' (N 3001, ht. 24.2 cm.); porter bottle, base moulded 'H. R. BRISTOL' (G 3225, ht. 25 cm.).
The shapes resemble those on the billhead of Henry Ricketts (TA 4628), only G 3583 showing the curved neck however.

Plate 41.

Plate 42.

Study of Flowers by Rolinda Sharples. c1825.
Oil on canvas. Signed 'Rolinda Sharples'. K 1086.
This Bristol painter illustrates a cut glass jug similar in style to those made by
William and Thomas Powell at the Red Lane glasshouse at this period. Robust in
shape, it shares the features of the two jugs by Powell's, G 605 and G 606: step-cut
and notched neck, fluted and hob-nail cut body, and thick loop handle.
See plate 35.

to contain, in imitation of the silver bottle tickets hung by a chain around a decanter's neck and carrying the name of the liquor. Quart-size labelled decanters cost Rhinelander 4s. 6d. Numerous references to engraved decanters occur in the merchant's papers, but patterns are not detailed. Rhinelander ordered 'fine Cut & Sprig'd' ones in 1776 and 1778 which presumably featured bands or sprays of floral sprigs. The 1779 order to Vigor and Stevens included three dozen 'fine Cut Quart Decanters very neat telescop'd.' This may refer to decanters with necks cut in deep horizontal bands. The following year, the New York importer ordered six decanters in a 'cut diamond' pattern, probably in response to a client's request. A rival merchant, Christopher Bancker, had advertised this same style of Bristol ware in 1774.[24]

For another special order for a set of glassware to be 'Cut with a star & beaded neat,' Rhinelander provided the Bristol firm with a pattern (plate 44). The drawing shows a decanter that has cut flutes around the base, a facet-cut neck, a band of tiny, cut beads in a wavy line around the body, and at least one large cut star. Included in this set were decanters in three sizes, carafes of pint size, half-pint glasses, three sizes of tumblers from gill to pint, lemonade cans, wines, and clarets. On January 25th, 1782, Rhinelander placed another order for a set of glassware, 'cut with a star & hanging border the same as last you sent.' Besides the forms already mentioned, he required two- and four-quart decanters and 'wash hand Glasses & Plates,' or finger bowls.

Wash hand glasses or basins first appear in a sales record of 1773; they are not mentioned in any of the orders to Bristol until 1779. This form was among the few that Rhinelander offered in coloured glass. From Vigor and Stevens he bought ones in white, blue, and purple glass. In 1780 he wanted blue and purple finger bowls that were 'scalloped & beaded.' The only other forms Rhinelander received in blue and purple were covered sugar bowls. In the 1779 order he specified that they be of a low, flat shape. Later, Rhinelander ordered engraved sugar bowls. It is possible that some moulded sugar basins and covers Rhinelander sold in 1774 were also made by Vigor and Stevens, although moulded glass does not appear in any of the orders or invoices. Blue glass salt liners and milk jugs were shipped to New York in 1780. 'Common' as well as fine engraved examples of the latter form were also provided by the factory at Redcliff Backs.

At his store on Burling's Slip, Rhinelander sold a full range of other serving pieces. Vigor and Stevens shipped him jelly glasses, bowls, salad bowls, salts, sweetmeat glasses, butter tubs, and cruet bottles of both common and cut varieties. Cruet bottles sent in 1773 were labelled in the manner of the decanters. Rhinelander ordered glass tea canisters in 1778, adding that they should have screw tops. Pickle plates are first listed in 1781. According to Rhinelander's instructions, they were to be long and *not* engraved.

Rhinelander had only a small business in glass lighting devices. In 1779 he ordered binnacle lamps for ships and lanterns for entries. Two years later he imported 'Globe lanthorns or barrel lamps.' Several sales of glass shades, either for wall lights or table candlesticks, were found in the sales volumes.

Although many of the sales records exist for the Rhinelander store, there is as yet no glass object known with a history that can be associated with one of Rhinelander's customers and, therefore, interpreted as an example of the Vigor and Stevens production from this period. At the New-York Historical Society, however, there is a collection of archaeological material gathered in the early twentieth century from the sites of British military barracks and the homes of leading Loyalists. Represented in this collection are plain and cut tumblers, and simple wineglasses with plain and twist stems.[25] Some of these glasses may have been made in Bristol and sold by Rhinelander.

On the whole, Frederick Rhinelander seems to have been pleased in his dealings with Vigor and Stevens. He lodged fewer complaints than with his pottery suppliers. On one occasion he asked that the cruets be 'neater than the last.' When he unpacked a shipment in 1789 the New York merchant found 'the present Ware is not so white and clear as we have had from you before.' Sometimes, mistakes were made. Vigor and Stevens sent Rhinelander some cut salad bowls he had not ordered. 'We had all the former parcell still on hand,' he wrote, '(which from their high price are rendered unsaleable here) we should by no means have wished to [have] received any more.'[26] With the styles and patterns the Bristol glasshouse selected Rhinelander was apparently satisfied. Most of his orders ended with a postscript to the effect that a few pieces of any 'New fashioned' glassware would always be acceptable. While Rhinelander often gave detailed packing instructions to his ceramics agents, he only reminded Vigor and Stevens to use 'good strong Crates,' pack the glass in the 'best manner,' and ship 'by means of the first Vessel that sails with the Convoy.' Sometimes he suggested they send their shipment merely with the first armed vessel out of port.

The Revolutionary War, of course, created delays and inconveniences in overseas trade. Letters and payments often took months to arrive at their destination, and, as mentioned earlier, cargoes were in danger from the raids of American privateers. Vigor and Stevens must have feared the remittances would not be forthcoming at all. That the Bristol manufacturers were willing to trade under such adverse circumstances indicates the importance of the American market to their business.

Rhinelander did his best to allay any fears on the part of his suppliers. Governor Tryon attested to the merchant's loyalty to the Crown in a letter which was circulated to various correspondents in England. On several occasions Rhinelander assured Vigor and Stevens that their debt with him was 'safe'. On November 12th, 1781, shortly after the surrender of Cornwallis at Yorktown, Rhinelander wrote to the Bristol firm that he had received their latest invoice for £903 12s. 6d., but the 'general stagnation of business & sudden rise of bills prevents our sending you any remittance for this conveyance. Although the misfortune of Lord Cornwallis will naturally allarm your Merchants who have property here, we beg leave however to assure you that your interest in our hands is perfectly safe and that our remittances shall be as regular as usual, and that no circumstances shall induce us to act otherwise.' Rhinelander continued to import and sell glass and china into 1783. Expecting the proclamation of peace at any moment, Rhinelander informed Vigor and Stevens that when peace was declared he intended to carry on his glass business. With the evacuation of British troops in November, 1783, however, Rhinelander was no longer protected. As a Loyalist his property was confiscated by the state of New York. When he was able to return to business it was only as a lumber retailer.

Thus Vigor and Stevens lost an important customer. Because they and the other glassmakers of Bristol relied so heavily on the export trade with North America and the Caribbean islands, the war with the American colonies affected their business very seriously in the 1770s and 1780s.[27] Their connections with merchants in all parts of America seem to have been renewed, however, in the 1790s. Shipping records document the involvement of Lucas and Company, Elton and Company, Lawson and Company, and Stevens, Cave, and Company with the Charleston, New York, and Boston markets.[28] Crown glass and bottles remained a significant part of the trade of this era.

'Elegant cut table glass from Bristol' was sold by such merchants as Charles Evans in New York. The prices of such quality ware can be documented in invoices of the Stevens Glass Concern found among the papers of a Baltimore merchant, Hugh Thompson. Sold in 1797 to T. and T. Powell, presumably on Thompson's behalf, were 24½ dozen items that were fluted and 'engraved to pattern.' These included decanters, champagne glasses, clarets, wines, wine coolers, finger basins, round cut jellies and syllabubs, and square cut rummers. The quart-size decanters with neck rings 'cut out' were the most expensive at 7s. 6d. apiece. At the same time, the Powells paid Isaac Jacobs £10 for '4 neat Elegant cut basons & covers' that were also intended for Thompson.[29]

In 1801 the Stevens Glass Concern consigned to Captain John Owens of the *Victory* a special order for glass placed by Josiah A. Fox, a Cornish man who became the chief clerk for General Henry Knox, America's first Secretary of War. At the time of the glass order, Fox was a private shipbuilder in Norfolk, Virginia. The set included four 'Quart Fluted Cutt ring'd decanters, Flower'd Star Pattern & Cyph[ere]d IAF' and water bottles and square foot tumblers to match.[30] A different set of 'cyphered' glass survives in two American museums that can be documented to Bristol (plate 45). William Smith, son of Boston merchant Isaac Smith, is known to have purchased the glass in Bristol in 1796. The set includes decanters, wines, tumblers, and rummers, each with the initials 'WS' engraved on a shield. Cut flutes decorate the bases and a band of small stars encircles each piece.[31]

In direct competition with such Bristol products were cheap, non lead tablewares manufactured in Bohemia and Germany. An extant trade catalogue of a Bohemian manufacturer illustrates their imitation of Anglo-Irish styles of cut and engraved glass.[32]

The Bristol industry also had to contend with America's own glasshouses and independent cutters and engravers, some of whom had made glass in Bristol. As early as 1709, a Bristol glassmaker, Daniel Tittery, proposed unsuccessfully to open a glasshouse in Philadelphia. Boston merchants also considered his plan but rejected it. Tittery's brother, Joshua, had been brought over from Newcastle-on-Tyne in 1683 to build a glassworks in Pennsylvania. The apparent failure of that undertaking was probably responsible for the lack of interest which met Daniel Tittery's idea.[33]

The Titterys were among the few Englishmen involved in the colonial glass industry. As mentioned earlier, most of the glassblowers employed in the dozen or so factories built in America in the seventeenth and eighteenth centuries were of Germanic origin. English influence began to be felt more strongly in the 1760s. About 1769 the secret of English lead

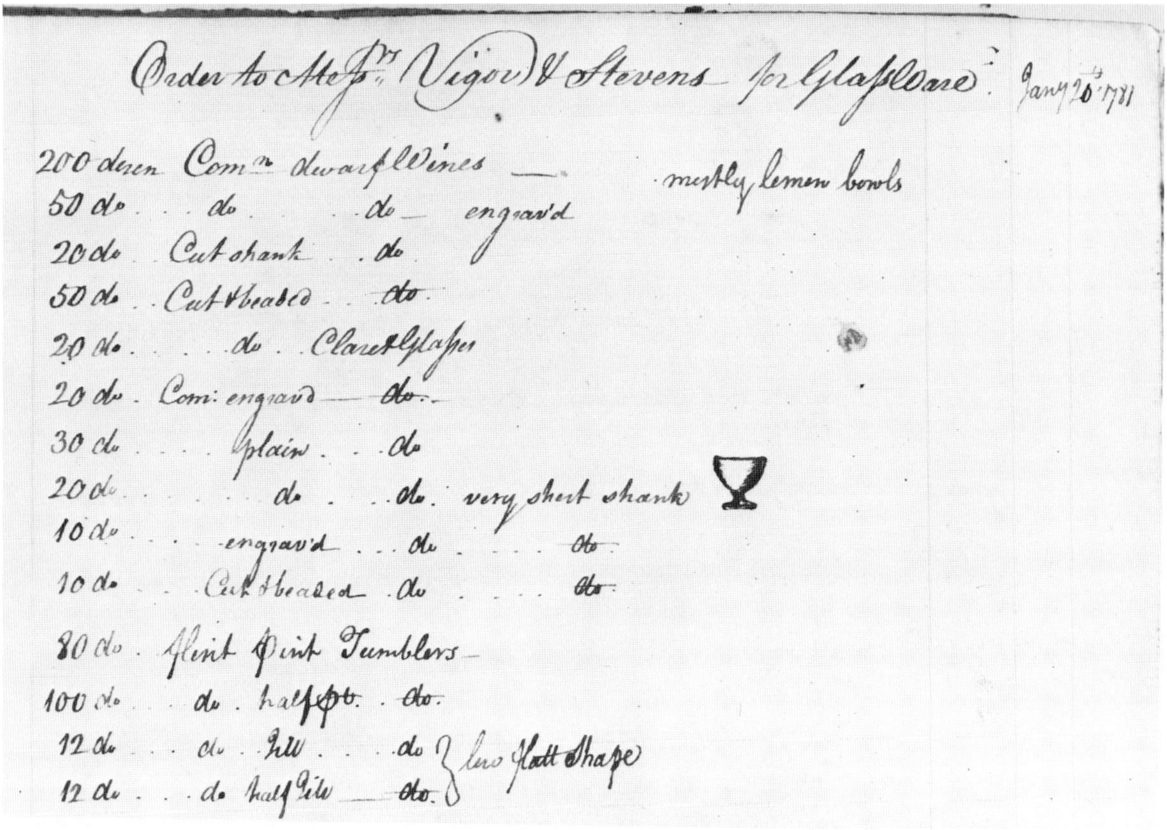

Order to Mess.rs Vigor & Stevens for Glassware. Jan.y 20.th 1781

200 dozen Com.n dwarf Wines _____   mostly lemon bowls
50 do. ... do. ... do_ engrav'd
20 do. Cut shank . do.
50 do. Cut & beaded .. do.
20 do. ... do. Claret Glasses
20 do. Com: engrav'd ___ do.
30 do. ... plain ... do
20 do. ... do. ... do. very short shank
10 do. ... engrav'd ... do. ... do.
10 do. ... Cut & beaded . do. ... do.

80 do. flint Pint Tumblers _____
100 do. ... do. half pt. . do.
12 do. ... do. Gill ____ do. } less Hatt shape
12 do. ... do. half Gill ____ do. }

Plate 43.

(Above) **Frederick Rhinelander's** "Order to Mess.rs Vigor & Stevens for Glass Ware Jany. 20 1781," with illustration of a plain claret glass "very short shank." Letter and Order Book, 1774–83, Frederick Rhinelander papers. Courtesy of the New-York Historical Society, New York City.

(Below) **Frederick Rhinelander's order to Vigor & Stevens,** September 15, 1780, with illustration of an oval-shape decanter, "Cut with a Star & beaded, neat." Letter and Order Book, 1774–83, Frederick Rhinelander Papers. Courtesy of the New-York Historical Society, New York City.

Plate 44.

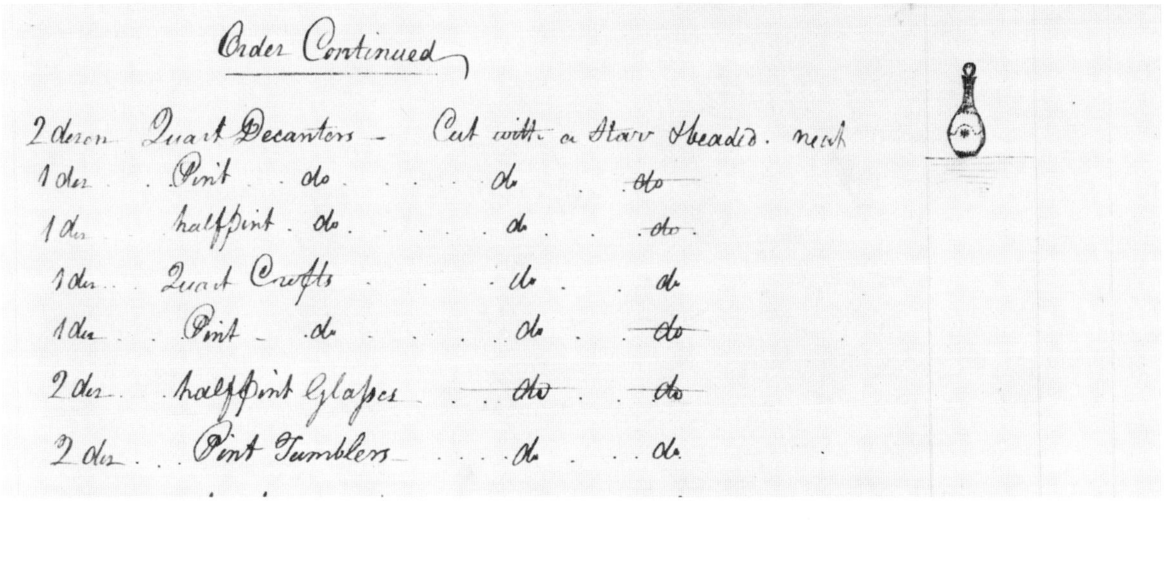

Order Continued

2 dozen Quart Decanters _ Cut with a Starr & beaded. neat
1 doz. Pint . do. ... do. do.
1 du. half pint. do. ... do. . do.
1 du. Quart Crafts ... do. . do.
1 du. Pint _ do. ... do. do.
2 du. half pint Glasses ... do. . do.
2 du. Pint Tumblers ... do. . do.

Plate 45.

Part of a set of table glass, each form with cut flutes, engraved stars and bands, and a shield bearing the initials "WS" for the original owner, William Smith of Boston, Massachusetts. The set was purchased in Bristol in 1796. Height of decanter, 29.8 cm. Courtesy, Portland Museum of Art, Portland, Maine, gift of Mrs. Eben Fox Corey.

glass was transferred to America, to the glassworks of Henry William Stiegel in Lancaster County, Pennsylvania. Although it has long been said that Stiegel himself made a trip to Bristol to engage workmen, firm proof of that visit has yet to be found. Certainly an Englishman named John Allman was hired; he seems to have been the one responsible for introducing lead glass.[34] His exact background in England has not yet been determined, but he may have been a descendant of the Weald glassmaker, John Alemayne.

Having failed to obtain sufficient recognition for his part in bringing the manufacture of 'White Flint Glass . . . to its Present Degree of Perfection,' Allman took his knowledge to a rival glass factory built in the Kensington section of Philadelphia in 1771. It is of this glassworks that William Logan wrote to Cornelius Fry, part owner of the Temple Street Flint Glassworks, Bristol, enclosing a sample of wineglasses produced at this Philadelphia venture.

> 'The Owners of this House tell me they are Well assured their next
> Glass will far exceed these now sent thee in Clearness as well as in
> other Respects, and We have some Glass Cutters lately Come over who
> cut Words—Grapes Coats of Arms or any Device that may be
> desired—This They do at less than I think is given in Bristol – Glasses
> cut at 14^d stg p Doz^n and Decanters with Grape Vines at $3\frac{1}{2}^d$ apce stg
> & So in pportion—Our Window Glass I am told but I have not Seen
> any of it Yet, exceeds yr Bristol Glass, but not the London Crown and
> They say They can and Will Sell it Cheaper y^n what is imported from
> Bristol can be bought at—These Glasses now sent I bo^t 2/– p Dozen
> lower than what is imported are sold for—If Your different
> manufacturers in England should be uneasy & think We may hurt
> them by getting too fast into different Manufactures, & We have
> Certainly gone much into them for these few Years past and find it
> Will answer Well They must thank Your Wise Administration for
> doing Every thing they Can to hamper & throw heavy Burdens on Our
> Trade—Which has been Greatly done for a few Years past The
> Americans will never forget the Intended Yoke of the Stamp Act—'[35]

Not only did the British glass manufacturers suffer from the increased duties on glass but also from the new threat of an American industry staffed with renegades from their own glasshouses. Frederick Rhinelander informed Vigor and Stevens in 1778 that

> 'A friend of ours in this business has got two Glass Cutters from
> England indented to him for three years, by which means he says his
> Cut Glass comes much lower than it can be imported. They are
> exceeding good Workmen. this branch of business will be lost to you at
> New York unless you can afford the Cut Glass something lower than
> usual, there is a great deal of Cut Glass used here at present.'[36]

One of the English glasscutters to whom Logan referred must have been Lazarus Issac who was the first glasscutter and engraver to advertise his talents in America. He briefly operated a cutting shop in Philadelphia early in 1773 before going to work for Stiegel. Efforts to trace his origins in England have not yet been successful, but it is possible that he was related to the Isaac Isaacs who is recorded as a glasscutter in Bristol in 1775.[37]

The British authorities tried to prevent the emigration of artisans to America, particularly in the post-Revolutionary period. One American glasshouse sent an agent to England to recruit workers in 1806. Tradition has it he was forced to dress as a beggar and could gain admittance to the glass factories only as a bag-pipe player. In 1815 five glassmakers were arrested as they boarded an America-bound ship at Liverpool.[38] One agent who 'came near being caught' but succeeded in hiring English glassblowers to travel to America was Charles F. Kupfer, acting on behalf of the Boston Glass Manufactory. The firm specifically wanted gaffers who knew how to make the thin Bristol crown glass. Among those Kupfer engaged was Thomas Cains (1779–1865), a man of Bristol training, who subsequently became the founder of the flint glass industry in New England.[39]

Born to a glassblower of Bolton parish, Gloucestershire, Cains apprenticed in Bristol at the Phoenix Glassworks of Wadham, Ricketts, and Company. He left there in March, 1812, and arrived in Boston the following month. On June 18th, 1812, America declared war on Great Britain. Because of the British blockade, the glasshouse was unable to get sand from its usual source in Demerara, British Guiana, so plans for this third window glass establishment of the Boston Glass Manufactory were set aside. Cains persuaded the management to build him a six-pot flint glass furnace at the South Boston facility and he commenced production in December. The earliest advertisements reveal that Cains was making only tumblers, in addition to apothecary and scientific glassware. None of it was probably flint. After the war, however, Cains was producing a full range of table glass of both moulded and cut varieties. In 1819 or 1820 he left the works to establish a factory of his own. He named it the Phoenix Glass Works after the Bristol one, and with only a brief, three-year retirement, Cains managed it until his death in 1865.

Several examples of free-blown glass were passed down in the Cains family and can be firmly attributed to Thomas Cains. One of them is shown in plate 46 . This sugar bowl is decorated with applied, triple-tooled bands on the cover and bowl. Set within the hollow knops of the finial and stem are Irish tenpence bank tokens of 1813. Another glass with a Cains history is a large footed mug, currently on loan to the Boston Museum of Fine Arts. It, too, has a bulbous knop in the stem enclosing a coin – an American quarter dollar of 1821. Around the base of the baluster-shaped body are five applied bands of glass pincered to form a chain. A number of other objects sharing these characteristics have surfaced in New England and have been attributed to Cains. The forms include two-handled cups, decanters, plates, bowls, and whale oil lamps. Some of these are encircled with what is known as a mercurial ring where air was trapped within an indented band around the piece.[40]

Besides these free-blown glasses, Cains is credited with examples of fully mould-blown wares of the kind made in England and Ireland. These include the 'blown over the mould' wares, mostly shallow dishes and salts made in one-piece, open moulds, and glasswares formed by blowing a gather into a three-part hinged mould. Indeed, Cains may well have introduced both of these techniques into America. The second method became an extremely popular means of shaping and decorating glass in America in the first half of the nineteenth century.

Although the present record is a patchy one, drawn from a miscellany of documents and objects, it is clear that an enormous quantity of Bristol's glass was destined for America. Bristol-made glass of all forms and qualities were known throughout the colonies, and then the republic. The volume and success of the trade, however, fluctuated with the political and financial climate, as did the fortunes of individual Bristol houses. For the nascent American glass industry of the late eighteenth and early nineteenth centuries, Bristol imports provided a standard of excellence to be emulated, and entrepreneurs sought Bristol-trained craftsmen who could ensure this standard was achieved. As America moved towards economic independence from Britain, her reliance on Bristol glass diminished. It is hoped that American libraries and collections will continue to yield information which will document more fully this complex relationship.

Notes

1. Exchequer Port Books, Bristol, 1740–58, Public Record Office, London, microfilm copy, M 266, Joseph Downs Manuscript and Microfilm Collection, Winterthur Museum, Winterthur, Delaware (hereafter DMMC); petition quoted in W. E. Minchinton, ed., *The Trade of Bristol in the Eighteenth Century,* Bristol Record Society Publications, vol.20 (Bristol, 1957), 46–47.

2. See Dwight P. Lanmon, 'The Baltimore Glass Trade, 1780 to 1820', *Winterthur Portfolio 5* (Charlottesville, Va.: University Press of Virginia, 1969), 15–49.

3. Powel Invoice Book, 54.83.19, DMMC; Sharp advertisement in *American Weekly Mercury* (Philadelphia) (July 11th–18th, 1734); Duykinck advertisement in *New York Mercury* (October 6th, 1766).

4. For a discussion of the Wistarburgh glassworks, see Arlene M. Palmer, 'Glass Production in Eighteenth-Century America: The Wistarburgh Enterprise,' *Winterthur Portfolio II* (Charlottesville, Va.: University Press of Virginia, 1976), 75–102.

5. Caspar Wistar Receipt Book, Historical Society of Pennsylvania, Philadelphia, Pa. (hereafter HSP). The correspondence cited here between Richard Wistar and the Taylor Glassworks and Freeman and Oseland is in the Richard Wistar Letterbook, private collection, microfilm copy M 220, DMMC.

6. Marshall advertisement in *Pennsylvania Journal* (September 8th, 1748). Christopher and Charles Marshall Account Book, 61.35, DMMC.

7. Vigor, Stevens and Hill broadside published in *Antiques,* 17 (March 1930): 262. Invoice, Vigor, Stevens, Randolph, and Stevens, September 9th, 1789, 74.195, DMMC.

8. Advertisement of J. Sherred in *New York Commercial Advertiser* (October 1st, 1810); Letter, Ebenezer Adams to George C. Shattuck, December 8th, 1810, Shattuck MSS, Massachusetts Historical Society, Boston, Mass.

9. *Portland Gazette* (September 21st, 1819); the prices on the New York market were published in the *Baltimore American* (July 28th, 1825).

10. Letter, Hugh Roberts to Charles Willing, May 27th, 1752, Charles Morton Smith MSS, vol.1, 117, HSP.

11. Banister advertisement, *Boston Newsletter* (June 9th–16th, 1712); Rodgers advertisements in *New York Evening Post,* references courtesy Neil Larson.

12. 1765 inventory, Philadelphia County Probate Records, microfilm M 1032, no. 243, DMMC; Master and Markoe advertisement in *New York Commercial Advertiser* (November 1st, 1830), quoted in Helen McKearin and Kenneth M. Wilson, *American Bottles and Flasks and Their Ancestry* (New York: Crown, 1978), p 231.

13. Mayer and Lohman advertisement in *Poulson's American Daily Advertiser* (March 3rd, 1825), advertisement of Boston Glass Bottle Company in *Boston Commercial Gazette,* quoted in Lura Woodside Watkins, 'Glassmaking in South Boston,' Part II, *Antiques* 48 (October 1945): 218–19.

14. December 29th, 1770, Marshall Account Book, p 127.

15. Regarding Robert Turlington, see Ivor Noël Hume, *Glass in Colonial Williamsburg's Archaeological Collections,* Colonial Williamsburg Archaeological Series no. 1 (Williamsburg: Colonial Williamsburg), pp 43–44.

16. That Banister vials were for a medicine known as Banister's drops is seen by another reference in the inventory taken of the estate of Hannah Hodge in 1736. Appraisers recorded '3 bottles of Banister's drops' worth £4 10s., and '15 small bottles ditto' at £1 2s. 6d. Philadelphia County Probate Records, microfilm M 1002, no. 3, DMMC.

17. *Boston Newsletter* (April 26th–May 4th, 1719), quoted in Kenneth M. Wilson, *New England Glass and Glassmaking* (New York: Crowell, 1972), p 13; DeBlois advertisement in *Boston Gazette* (June 8th, 1761).

18. The Frederick Rhinelander Papers at the New-York Historical Society, New York City, comprise twenty-five volumes of letter and order books, day books, sales ledgers, memo books, and miscellaneous volumes. They will hereafter be cited as FRP. A paper concerning Rhinelander's glass trade was delivered by the author at the International Glass Conference at the Corning Museum of Glass, June, 1982, and subsequently published: 'English Glass Imports in New York, 1770–1790,' *Journal of Glass Studies*, 25 (1983), 179–85. An article discussing Rhinelander's ceramics trade will be published by the author in 1984: 'The Ceramic Imports of Frederick Rhinelander, New York Loyalist Merchant,' *Winterthur Portfolio* (Spring, 1984).

19. Other importing merchants in New York City were George Ball, James Gilliland, and James and Arthur Jarvis.

20. Rhinelander to Perrin, December 28th, 1776; Rhinelander to Kenyon, October 14th, 1778; Rhinelander to John Hill, August 30th, 1780, in Letter and Order Book, 1774–84, FRP.

21. The 1772 invoice from Richard Cannington totalled £163 3s.6½d., but was not paid by Rhinelander until February 27th, 1775. The invoice itself is not extant, only the record of its payment, in Daybook, 1774–77, p 71; Rhinelander to Vigor and Stevens, March 21st, 1778, Letter and Order Book, 1774–84, FRP.

22. Drawings of claret glasses accompany the September 15th, 1780, and January 20th, 1781, orders, Letter and Order Book, 1774–84, FRP.

23. Examples are known engraved, 'THE KING & THE FRIENDS OF HIS MAJESTYS AMERICAN LOYALISTS,' and matching wines with other wartime inscriptions. See Wadsworth Atheneum, *Glass from Six Centuries,* comp. Dwight P. Lanmon (Hartford, Conn.: Wadsworth Atheneum, 1978), p 61, fig. 59.

24. Bancker advertisement in *Supplement, New York Gazette* (June 13th, 1774).

25. Reginald Pelham Bolton, 'Porcelain, Pottery and Glass, Cast Away by the Soldiery in the War of Independence,' *The New-York Historical Society Quarterly Bulletin* 13, no. 3 (October 1929); 87–110.

26. Rhinelander to Vigor and Stevens, August 30th, 1780 and January 25th, 1782, Letter and Order Book, 1774–84, FRP.

27. See Cyril Weeden, 'The Ricketts Family and the Phoenix Glasshouse, Bristol,' *The Glass Circle 4*, eds. R. J. Charleston, Wendy Evans, Ada Polak (London: Gresham Books, 1982), 85, 91.

28. Minchinton, pp 57–59.

29. Evans advertisement in *New York Commercial Advertiser* (September 22nd, 1800); Invoice, Stevens Glass Concern to T. & T. Powell, July 10th, 1797, and Invoice, Isaac Jacobs to T. & T. Powell, July 8th, 1797, Hugh Thompson MSS, Maryland Historical Society, photostat copies 1103.19, .25, DMMC.

30. 'Early Glass Documents,' *Antiques* 40 (August 1941): 102–103. Billhead is illustrated.

31. The Smith decanter from the Boston Museum of Fine Arts collection is illustrated and discussed in Kathryn C. Buhler, 'Recent Accessions in Boston,' *Antiques* 73 (January 1957): 52,53.

32. These catalogues, in the collection of the Winterthur Museum Library, are known as The Gardiner Island Trade Catalogues. They were published and discussed in Lanmon, 'The Baltimore Glass Trade.'

33. Thomas Fitch to Edward Shippen, August 15th, 1709, Thomas Fitch Letterbook, 1702–11, American Antiquarian Society, Worcester, Mass.

34. T. Kenneth Wood, 'A Gratuity for Baron Stiegel,' *Antiques* 7 (January 1925): 30.

35. William Logan to Cornelius Fry, May 17th [1773], Smith Papers, Library Company of Philadelphia.

36. Rhinelander to Vigor and Stevens, May 17th, 1778, Letter and Order Book, FRP.

37. Isaac advertised in *Pennsylvania Packet* (May 17th, 1773); the Bristol glasscutter is mentioned in Francis Buckley, *A History of Old English Glass* (London: Ernest Benn Ltd., 1925), p 140.

38. The bag-pipe playing agent was sent by the Rensselaer Glass Factory, Sandlake, New York, according to Arthur J. Wiese, *History of the 17 Towns of Rensselaer County* (Troy, N.Y., 1880), pp 136–37; news of the Liverpool arrest was published in the *Raleigh* (North Carolina) *Star* (December 22nd, 1815).

39. For information on Thomas Cains, see Wilson, *New England Glass and Glassmaking*, pp 198–213; Lura Woodside Watkins, 'Glassmaking in South Boston,' Part I, *Antiques* 48 (September 1945): 140–43.

40. The mug is illustrated in Wilson, *New England Glass and Glassmaking*, p 214, fig. 163. For illustrations of other Cains forms, see pp 210–26.

Plate 46.

Sugar bowl, with applied, tooled horizontal bands and hollow knops in the stem and finial, each containing an Irish tenpence bank token of 1813. Made at the South Boston Flint Glass Works of Thomas Cains, 1813–29. Cains had been trained at the Phoenix Glassworks in Bristol. The bowl descended in the Cains family. Height 23.8 cm. Courtesy, Corning Museum of Glass, Corning, New York, gift of Dr. Malcolm Johnston.

CLEO WITT

Cleo Witt took her degree in classics at the University of Cambridge, then trained in textile conservation and joined the Worcester County Museum as decorative arts assistant. She came to Bristol as assistant curator of applied art and is now curator. She has lectured widely on the decorative arts and on ceramics, in this country and in the U.S.A., and is a member of the English Ceramic Circle and the Glass Circle, and a Fellow of the Museums Association. She has a keen interest in glass, having recently co-selected the exhibition 'British Art Glass' of contemporary glass.

CYRIL WEEDEN

Cyril Weeden trained as an engineer in the aircraft industry and later read for an external degree in economics at London University, specialising in sociology. He subsequently joined the Council of Industrial Design, with responsibility for the glass exhibits at the Festival of Britain. In 1953 he went to the Glass Manufacturers Federation to inaugurate the information services, market research and development. Retirement provides the opportunity for following his interest in the history of the glass industry. He is a Fellow of the Society of Antiquaries, and a Fellow of the Society of Glass Technology.

ARLENE PALMER SCHWIND

From 1973 to 1979 Arlene Palmer Schwind was the curator of glass and ceramics at the H. F. du Pont Winterthur Museum in Delaware. The role of glass imported into America before 1850 and the rise of America's glass industry have been the focus of her research and publications. Currently she is preparing a catalogue of Winterthur's glass collection.